Simple
Logical
Repeatable

Systemise like McDonald's to scale, sell
or franchise your growing business

Marianne Page

Praise for *Simple, Logical, Repeatable*

"What an easy-to-read and inspirational book! As an entrepreneur with a growing business, I loved the concept of *Simple, Logical, Repeatable* from the outset and started off highlighting the *bons mots* that stood out for me. I was looking for top tips, insights or even moments of absolute clarity about my business and soon found that I was highlighting most paragraphs! As well as excellent business planning and strategy ideas, there are wonderful metaphors throughout to bring these alive, and plenty of humour too. The author reminds us: 'What we do today, creates our future' and with that in mind, what you need to do today, in my opinion, is buy this book!"

JANE MALYON
CEO, The English Cream Tea Company

"Marianne has taken her considerable experience with McDonald's and translated it into her own model, helping successful business owners to step back from the day to day, and become both consistent and high performing. She has helped me bring out my team, and let them truly develop. Her 'McFreedom System' has helped transform my business, and freed up my time to focus on growing it."

JEFFREY LERMER
Founder and Managing Director Jeff Lermer & Associates

"After reading Marianne's book (and subsequently attending her training) I now have the blueprint for ensuring that my business supports my life instead of my life (long hours, no holidays, staffing issues taking priority over home life), supporting my business. As an entrepreneur, my dream was to have the freedom to live my life the way I wanted to, but the more successful my business became the less time I had for the things that mattered. Now I know the simple changes I need to make in order to get my life back."

HEENA THAKER
CEO, Bee in Company

"As a young entrepreneur, everyone told me to read *The E-myth*. I did. But I didn't get it. Now finally Marianne Page shows us creative entrepreneurial types not just why we need a simple, logical, repeatable approach – but gives us the how to. And, dare I say it, she makes it fun. A must read for every entrepreneur looking to scale, sell, or just get their life back."

DR JOANNA MARTIN
Founder, One of many and EMPRESS global collective

"I love this book. It's conversational and enjoyable to read yet every page is packed with game changing ways to get a business running powerfully. Marianne really gives generously in this book sharing insights from her 20+ years in senior leadership roles at McDonald's. She breaks it down step-by-step and talks about what's needed to duplicate a business into 35,000+ locations. Reading this book gave me a burst of energy and renewed vision for how my business could scale even faster and more reliably around the world serving more people."

DANIEL PRIESTLEY
Best-selling business author and founder of Dent Global.

"This book is an essential read for any business owner who wants to further their success in a *'Simple, Logical and Repeatable'* way, and to free them up to focus on what's important to them. There are loads of useful exercises and from doing these a step-by-step plan can be implemented to get immediate results. What I love about this book is that while it focuses on your business, it is importantly also about helping you as a person, leader, business owner and family member, to achieve the freedom to live your life and be the success you want to be."

TRESSANDRA HENDERSON
Former Group HR Director, TBWA UK Group

"As a small business owner operating in a franchised type legal business, I couldn't initially see how Marianne's famous 'systems and processes' would fit into my personal business. After reading *Simple, Logical, Repeatable*, I'm starting to look at everything I do differently. This book is not only about business but beautifully weaves in vital considerations around mindset and values – bringing business and life together, as they should be. My favourite quote, 'if a system isn't working in your business, it's the wrong system' could equally be applied to our lives. Marianne might just change the way (and the why) business is done, for the better."

HANNAH BEKO
Partner, gunnercooke llp

"I'm not a fan of McDonald's. But then the McFreedom System isn't about burgers, it's about Marianne caring enough to give business owners a recipe for freedom and success. As business owners, we have essentially two roads to freedom. One is to create a business that delivers value without us, and the other is to create a business where we only do the tasks we love, both of which require systems and a team. If you need help implementing simple, logical and repeatable systems, then on the evidence of what's in these pages, there are few people better equipped than Marianne to guide you."

ALAN LEWIS
Values Trainer, Speaker & Author

Dent. | Books

Cartoons by Andrew Priestley

Contents

CHAPTER 6
McFreedom   191

This book is dedicated to my mum and dad

Mum - thank you for your love, for the sacrifices you made to bring me into the world and for giving me the courage and determination to live a life truly fulfilled.

Dad - thanks for giving me your optimism, your desire to make a positive difference to the lives of those I meet and your ability to bounce back from any body blow or disappointment. I've needed that once or twice!

The gifts you've both given me have made me who I am, and although neither of you are here to see this book, I know you would be proud.

Foreword

At age 15 I was living a double life. As far as my parents knew, I was incapable of cleaning my room, doing dishes or staying on top of my homework. Meanwhile at my after-school McDonald's job I had progressed to the rank of "Crew Trainer" and was responsible for a small team. I would run the kitchen, producing thousands of dollars of food per hour. I would serve customers and leave them feeling delighted. I would leave the store, proud that it was spotless and ready for the next shift.

All of this was made possible by the McDonald's systems for training, operations, management and marketing.

My three years at McDonald's gave me my first taste of business and got me hooked on the idea that one day I would create a scalable business that ran like clockwork. When I first met Marianne Page and learned of her experience, I enthusiastically shared my passion for the McDonald's business model.

I'm absolutely thrilled that she's captured some of the best ideas from her time as a senior leader and put it into this book. I'm even more thrilled to be able to publish it.

I love this book. It's conversational and enjoyable to read yet every page is packed with game-changing ways to get a business running powerfully. Marianne really gives generously in this book, sharing insights from her 20+ years in senior leadership roles at McDonald's. She breaks it down step-by-step and talks about what's needed to duplicate a business into 35,000+ locations – it's remarkably more straightforward than I thought.

Reading this book gave me a burst of energy and renewed vision for how my business could scale even faster and more reliably around the world, serving more people. I feel very lucky to have had a first look at this manuscript – this is going to help a lot people grow their small businesses. I'm going to give copies of this book to friends and clients.

DANIEL PRIESTLEY
FOUNDER OF DENT GLOBAL

Preface

An entrepreneur went to see a wily old investor to ask her to fund his business idea. He had a brilliant idea about a product he wanted to launch, and he felt sure she would be interested in helping him.

The investor sat patiently while the entrepreneur enthused about his business plan, going through his proposal in great detail.

When he'd finished, the investor sat back and smiled knowingly. She agreed that the entrepreneur had a great product and that it had real potential, 'but', she told the entrepreneur, 'you've made the mistake that so many entrepreneurs make. You've missed a key element out of your plan, and without this your plan will fail. So on that basis, I'm afraid I can't fund your business.'

The entrepreneur was completely taken aback. He knew he had a good product, and it was already selling well. Recognising his dejection, and admiring the passion he had for his business, the investor decided to help out and give him some free advice before he left.

'Do you think you can make better burgers than the ones that the McDonald's on the retail park make?' The entrepreneur wasn't sure where the investor was going with this, but he humoured her with a reply. 'Well there's no chance I could,' he said, 'but my mum, she can make burgers that are miles better than them.'

'Ok,' said the investor, 'have you tasted better burgers around where you live?'

'Of course I have,' said the entrepreneur. 'There are loads of places that serve better burgers than McDonald's. But what are you getting at?'

'Every entrepreneur tells me that they've tasted better burgers than McDonald's. So if that's the case, if so many other people do better burgers than McDonald's, if they're not really the best then how is it that there's no other burger business bigger than McDonald's? Not even close to them?'

A little confused, and still smarting from the rejection of his plan, the entrepreneur sensed that this must have something to do with his pitch, but was damned if he knew what it was. 'I've no idea,' he said. 'Why is that?'

'It's because McDonald's is not about the burgers. You get better burgers in lots of other places. McDonald's is all about consistency. It's all about systems, people, and consistent delivery of their product and customer experience, millions of times a day, all over the world. You buy a Big Mac anywhere in the world and it'll be the same size, have the same ingredients, and the same great (in my opinion) taste. What McDonald's have done is create a template for their product and service that works better than the vast majority of other brands. Customers go to McDonald's expecting the McDonald's experience, and they get it consistently, every day, no matter which McDonald's in the world they visit. That's something that your mum, and all the other restaurants that serve great burgers, haven't been able to, or choose not to replicate.'

'So what can I learn from them?' asked the entrepreneur, completely enthralled.

'You've got a great product,' said the investor, 'but without the consistent, reliable delivery that comes through having systems in every area of your business, you have no scalability. Any growth is reliant on you being there, on you being responsible for delivery. If you want to expand to anywhere else in the country, let alone overseas, your customer's experience won't be the same in terms of your product, or your service.

Having great products is essential for your business success, but it's your systems that will differentiate you and ensure your business growth.

My advice to you? Aim to become the McDonald's for your product.'

At that, she got up and left the entrepreneur to reflect on this game-changing guidance.

Introduction

What is this book about?

This book is about you taking the ACTION necessary to build a successful business that is completely in harmony with your successful life – having both the time and financial freedom to make real choices.

It's about moving from a 'great little business' to a 'proper business' with a great employer brand and a bottom line to match, that others want to model, copy and work with.

It's about learning from the best in the world how to take your successful small, and relatively insignificant business, and grow it into an empire – if that's what you want.

It's about you modelling the foundations of McDonald's success:

- ▸ their amazing consistency
- ▸ their ability to take a moody sixteen-year-old who wouldn't dream of washing a dish or tidying their room at home, and turn them into a productive and positive team member within weeks
- ▸ their genius in developing high performing teams, who follow simple systems to deliver exacting high standards

Why model McDonald's?

You know, people bitch about McDonald's all the time – see them as the Corporate monster – the sole reason that the western world is obese – the manipulative Happy Meal child catcher.

What everyone forgets is that McDonald's was once a little restaurant in the backwaters of California, smaller than your business is today, maybe. If they'd stayed that size, nobody would have hated them, just as no-one hates your business right now. Not that many people would have even known they existed, just as (with all due respect) not that many people know your business exists right now.

So what turned this business – this huge corporation made up of 36,000 small businesses – into the business that so many love to hate, the business that polarises views the world over?

The simple truth is that the founder, Ray Kroc, chose to do what we all love to talk about doing; to do what so many who've read *The E Myth* ponder over; he 'worked *on* the business, not *in* it.'

Ray Kroc wanted to build a restaurant system that would provide food of consistently high quality using uniform methods of preparation. He wanted to serve burgers, buns, fries and beverages that tasted just the same in Alaska as they did in Alabama.

So he developed systems that would run the business, and people who would run the systems, then he did it again, and again, and again, until his one restaurant became two, then five, then ten – on and on until one became 36,000, and counting.

This book is about you doing a Ray Kroc, and developing consistently high quality products and services, using consistent and uniform methods.

It's about you taking the *action* necessary to free up your time to work *on* your business.

It's about giving you the foundations and the freedom to scale, grow, sell or franchise your business... or run it from a beach somewhere, if that's what you want to do.

That's the definition of McFreedom. It's what The McFreedom System® is all about.

Who is it for?

It's for you, if:

- ▸ you're a successful seven figure business owner stuck working *in* your business
- ▸ you're an ambitious six figure business owner wanting to accelerate your growth
- ▸ you want to franchise, or perhaps sell your business; or
- ▸ you're a start-up who wants to start right!

I'm pretty sure you'll identify with one or more of our Usual Suspects too:

Stress-Head Stephen

You're frustrated and stressed almost all the time. There's so much to do and you're working longer and harder to get it all done.

Yes, your work is really important to you, but you're sick of it being your whole life.

You started with nothing, and here you are with a successful six, maybe seven-figure business, but you're not running it, it's running you.

You used to love what you do so much, and you do still enjoy making money, but success has led to a bigger team, and with more people have come more headaches. It was so much better when you were small and everyone just knew what they were doing. Now you're all over the place, with everybody doing things in their own way.

It's driving you mad.

Time Poor Teddie

You dreamt of having a business that gave you financial freedom. Now you have financial freedom, but you don't have time freedom to enjoy your money. Cash rich and time poor, as they say.

You've thought about selling up, but if you're going to do that, you know you need to make your business scalable, to develop a second line of managers who you trust to run the business in the way you would, without you looking over their shoulder. But that seems a million miles away at the minute.

If you could achieve that level of freedom though, then even if you don't choose to sell, you'll be able to step back from the day-to-day operation and have fun with other projects.

If only there was more than one of you.

Gertrude Gerber

You've read *The E-Myth*, and every other business book that tells you to work *on* your business, not *in* it – but you don't know where to start.

You've lost count of the number of online programmes you've bought, and courses you've attended, and your head is full of theory – of what you should be doing. But nothing has given you a practical How-To guide for systemising your business and making your life easier.

You're drowning in a sea of self-help, and need someone to teach you to swim.

Driven Dave

You want to accelerate your business growth – to scale, to franchise or maybe even to sell, BUT know you haven't got the right foundations in place.

You know you need to get the team performing well, and to have consistency in your operation, but you don't know where to start. You don't have time to create a million and one processes – you're way too busy running the business.

The same goes for plans – you know the numbers you want to achieve every year, and you know that if you work hard enough you'll achieve them – your people just have to keep up and deliver what you tell them to and you'll be ok, right?!

What you really want is someone just to show you how to sort this out and get your people working like a team; to have the business running like a well-oiled machine.

McDonald's have this sorted. Their people do the same things in the same way, every day, everywhere. They're amazingly consistent. The way they work is scalable.

You get it.

That's why you're here!

NB – It's not for you if you're in love with the struggle; if you believe all the myths (detailed in Chapter 1) around process and systems and think they're not worth the effort. I can get you past the language, but if your mindset is that systems are a luxury (and I say this with love) give this book to someone else.

Why this book?

Because I'm just like you.

I understand what you're going through. Yes, I spent a lot of years in the corporate world, working with business owners like you, but then I started my own business and just like you I've built it from the ground up on passion and hard work; faced the same problems you've faced, struggled with the same challenges.

Successful small business owners all have one thing in common – the desire for an easier life. Not a lazy life, just an easier life. A life where we have more freedom; where we're not working seventy-hour weeks; where we're not always checking up on someone; where we have no guilt because we have work-life harmony, with lots of quality time to spend with our family and friends.

The sort of life you're after, right?

Systems make life easier – if they don't, they're the wrong systems.

I learned of their power way before I joined McDonald's.

I was the fifth of my parents' six daughters – when my youngest sister was born, my eldest was only eleven, so you can bet your life my mum had systems.

Systems for getting us up, dressed and out to school. Systems for getting our chores done – beds made, toys tidied, dishes washed – even if it meant standing on a biscuit tin to reach the sink.

My older sisters, at eleven, ten and nine, were taught to help their little sisters; to lay out vest, pants and socks at the end of the bed, like Snow White and the Seven Dwarves, ready for the morning. Big red pants from M&S as I recall – I can still picture them now, hanging together on the washing line!

I learned the power of teamwork, delegation and systems before my sixth birthday, from a woman who, without them, might have crumbled under the weight of being a mother and home-maker for six little girls, while managing the sales and admin for my dad's growing coal business.

Mum understood that the best way to have time to do the things that only you can do, is to give ownership and responsibility for the rest to others; to have a system, and to train your team, whatever their age, to follow it to your high standard. McDonald's founder, Ray Kroc, would have loved my mum! Because what Mum taught us as kids is what you learn at McDonald's: replace yourself and free your time.

It's a very simple formula: develop systems to run every aspect of your business, develop a high performing team to run them, and then get out of their way.

That's how McDonald's have grown from one small restaurant to thousands and thousands all over the world: by developing their people, and having them replace themselves over and over and over again.

Systems run the business, and good people run the systems. It's the McDonald's model and it works.

So why don't more businesses copy it?

Why do so many businesses end up with a chaotic and complicated operation, where everyone is going in roughly the same direction, but in their own way and at their own speed; when what they set out to be was a Formula One operation – a high performing team where everyone knows exactly what they are doing, how it fits into the bigger picture, and that they are responsible for doing it to a high standard?

McDonald's are a Formula One operation and whatever your views on them, it's vital that you recognise that they have the recipe for the sort of success you're looking for.

Just look around you and you'll find evidence of how they have scaled, grown, franchised, and even made it possible for franchisees to pretty much run their business from the beach, if they choose to.

Gertrude has this much right – *The E-Myth* gave you a simple but brilliant formula for success: work *on* your business not *in* it. This book gives you a hefty dose of the how – and the what, why, who and when too. Because they're all important.

It's a blueprint for modelling McDonald's.

How to use this book

I recommend that you read the book all the way through to get the big picture, to make sure that you understand the four foundations of The McFreedom System®, and to see how the four foundations are interlinked – all reliant on one another to make one powerful whole.

It's so important that you get the necessity of having systems in every area of your business – planning, hiring, training, performance management, as well as in your day-to-day operation, if you want it to run like clockwork, without you being there.

So many business owners come to me saying, 'Oh can you just look at our operating processes, we don't need that people bit, we have HR.' The same people will often have an operations manual full of operating procedures that sits on a shelf somewhere, unused.

If you want a business that is run by a highly engaged, high performing team, without you being there, then you need all four foundations, working as one.

So read the whole book once right though, and then complete your **Business Sale or Scalability Indicator,** via this link:

mariannepage.co.uk/getstarted

Through a series of yes/no questions, the indicator will assess where you're at right now with each of the foundations, and give a score for each that will help you to understand which areas need most immediate attention.

Then go back and focus on each area, one at a time. Remember, focus is the key – focus and baby steps taken every day. Try to do everything at once, and there's every chance you'll see this as an overwhelming task and just give up.

FOCUS AND BABY STEPS.

How the book works

The book is split into five main sections, four covering each of the foundations of The McFreedom System® and the final section looking at you, your mindset, and what's required to make McFreedom a reality for you.

In each section you will find:

1. A foreword about why this foundation is important, and how McDonald's approached it

2. The key content broken down into manageable chunks complete with exercises and challenges

3. A summary of the key takeaways

4. A call to Do One Thing – *Today!*

All set? Then let me introduce you to...

—

CHAPTER 1

The McFreedom System®

What is The McFreedom System® and where did it come from?

As you know now, I pretty much grew up at McDonald's, and spent the majority of my adult life, as a senior manager, working with their systems, developing my own, and building high performing teams capable of delivering consistently excellent results.

It was simply, 'the way we did things,' at Macs.

When I left, and began working with small businesses, I realised that there were a lot of things I had taken for granted. I'm not talking about being able to turn to any member of a large team to get something done, although that was a big miss in the early days! What I'm talking about are the systems and structure that I had been so used to, which were not only missing, but also not considered to be essential.

Like my dad, most successful small business owners are self-taught and self-made: entrepreneurs who build their business on grit, determination and hard work, from the ground up. They start on their own, or with a small team, and achieve six- or seven-figure revenues without any real structure or solid foundations in place.

As revenues rise, the team grows, the people-pain builds and the cracks begin to appear. So they work harder, they stay later, they cancel holiday plans, and the business begins to run them rather than the other way round. What I saw were lots of successful people caught in the cycle of stress and long hours.

Some had worked out that there had to be an easier way, and were actively looking for it. Some, you could tell, never would.

It made me reflect on how I'd worked at Macs – what it was about McDonald's that just worked; what they had in place that made life easier, that freed their leaders and managers to do just that – lead and manage.

I analysed the way they did things, the way they got things done. I worked out the essential elements, thinking about what worked brilliantly, and what could work a little better with a slight tweak. I recognised that McDonald's have a system for everything – from initial training for team members, to how you stack boxes of fries in the freezer – but that nobody really talks about systems, they're just part of the business DNA, simply 'the way we do things round here'.

I wrote a book, *Process to Profit*, to share what I'd learned at the time but, helpful as I'm told that book is (one five-star reviewer hailed it as 'better than *The E Myth*'), I hadn't quite nailed the model. It needed more structure, focus and clarity to be the sort of blueprint that any business could use. So I spread my wings a bit further, working with successful small businesses from professional services to manufacturing, from consultancy to cleaning, to test out what I'd learned, listening to their feedback, fine-tuning and shaping the model that would hit the mark.

And so, The McFreedom System® was born – the blueprint that will free you to scale, grow, sell or franchise your business – or run it from a beach somewhere.

I named it McFreedom with an affectionate and respectful nod to McDonald's who inspired it, and Freedom, because that's exactly what it will give you and your team.

For your team – freedom from you looking over their shoulders all the time, checking up on them, re-doing their work; giving them the confidence to take ownership of their role and the ability to perform it to a high standard.

For you – freedom to work *on* the business rather than slogging away *in* it, allowing you to focus on what you do best, able to fully trust that your team are taking care of the day-to-day – running the systems that are running your business, giving you time – and the freedom to choose what you do with it.

The System is modelled on the foundations that have underpinned McDonald's success for sixty years and counting – the foundation systems that have made them unbelievably consistent, reliable and trusted in the global marketplace.

The foundations that will do the same for you.

Planning – your planning system – the clarity around your destination and your route map to get you there; your personal management system – your values, your leadership, and how you manage yourself day-to-day.

Process – your customer journey and the operating processes that support it: how simple and straightforward is your customer's journey through your business; is there a system in every area of the business, and is each one simple, logical and repeatable?

People – your hiring system – ensuring you hire the right people first time; your training system – teaching every team member 'how we do things round here' and the consistently high standards you expect.

Performance – the measurement and management of team and individual performance – keeping everyone on track;

business performance measurement and management – understanding that you have CPIs (critical performance indicators) as well as KPIs (key performance indicators), and staying on top of both.

Four essential systems that form the foundation of any business looking to grow or scale.

The McFreedom System® is your blueprint for building a highly engaged, high performing team.

It's a practical model for business growth and scale; a continuous cycle of improvement; a way of doing business – a change of style.

It's not a 'do once and stick in a drawer' sort of system. It's about making 'the way we do things round here' simple, logical and repeatable, developing routines, habits and systems that make everyone's life easier – yours, your customers', your team's.

It's a model that works for McDonald's, and it will work for you.

SYSTEMS MAY NOT BE SEXY BUT THE RESULTS THEY DELIVER ARE!

Busting the myths around systems

Maybe you're still a doubter – we're talking systems here, right? And while we all have systems, talking about them (or their little brother Process) rarely inspires or excites.

In fact, they're like a dog with a bad name, which is plain crazy when the truth is that systems create the space between the business owner and their business that allows them to control it, work on it and grow it.

So, let's bust a few of the myths and misconceptions and elevate systems to the status they deserve.

Myth 1: Systems stifle creativity

I hear this a lot. 'Oh we're a business that relies on our people being creative and free-flowing; systems would restrict us.'

Not true, in fact quite the reverse. Systems keep the nuts and bolts of your business – your invoicing, purchasing, marketing – moving, and form a platform for the creative people to do their stuff.

Think of a jazz band – you would never say that jazz musicians are not creative, or that in any piece of jazz music there isn't plenty of room for improvisation and individuality – but as a band, they all have to play in the same key, they all have to maintain the overall rhythm, and stick to the same beat.

Myth 2: Systems are a luxury that only large organisations need

Any business that wants to grow, whatever their size, needs systems and processes.

Revisit Michael Gerber's *The E Myth* – 'the only way to grow your business is to work *on* it, not *in* it.' The only way to have the time and control to work *on* your business is to have your team working to consistent systems and measurable standards.

Myth 3: Systems are dull and boring

Systems are simply 'the way we do things around here', so they're as exciting or dull as your business!

In other words, we all have systems, but we may not label them as such, which means they are probably not efficient or standardised. Having simple, logical and repeatable systems is liberating because you and your team don't have to think about how you're going to do something today, you just do it on autopilot, following your system.

Myth 4: Systems are all about Lean and Six Sigma

Lean systems thinking and Six Sigma are well established methods of increasing efficiency, particularly in manufacturing, and have done an enormous amount to make business more cost efficient and productive; but they have made process management sound bureaucratic, difficult and a lot of additional hard work. All the jargon and the academic-sounding terms have made people think that putting systems in place is going to be painful.

The most important thing to focus on is that simple, logical and repeatable systems will lower your costs, improve your revenue and ensure that you build a high performing team.

Myth 5: Having systems costs money

While it's true that you have to spend time and money getting your systems in place – and a little more at regular intervals to make sure that they are still relevant and effective – having systems will save you much more than they will ever cost.

And they will grow your revenue too, by helping you build a high performing team that delivers a great customer experience.

> **SYSTEMS EXIST TO MAKE OUR LIVES EASIER, THERE IS NO OTHER REASON FOR THEM. IF A SYSTEM DOESN'T MAKE LIFE EASIER, IT'S THE WRONG SYSTEM.**

CHAPTER 2

Foundation #1 Planning

The journey begins.
Are we there yet?

Planning as a cornerstone of McDonald's success

When Ray Kroc was building McDonald's he started with a big vision and then built the plans that would get him there.

What I learned at McDonald's is that planning is a team sport; most effective when it involves the people it affects as well as those who will deliver on it. Add someone with no bias or axe to grind into the mix, and you will develop a truly effective plan.

I learned that you listen to those with the skills and experience, but you also consider the new and the different; that it's ok to re-visit what might once have been considered crazy or just plain wrong for the business, as things change and the 'right time' comes along.

Just like every other area of the business, I learned that you have a system for planning that makes it routine, regular, consistent, and keeps you focused on the end goal, even when you need to adapt, or change your route.

A robust planning system keeps everyone in the business focused and on track. Since everyone knows where you're all headed, there is less stress, and less chaos, which also saves you time and money. And it gives you the opportunity to celebrate with your team when you reach your milestone markers along the way.

McDonald's teams all over the world still have that big vision at the heart of their plans. They are still focused on the question: What are we trying to achieve, and why? At every level – from the top, to your local restaurant – plans are developed in line with the vision for the business, with franchisees, corporate teams, and even suppliers invited to contribute.

McDonald's want everyone to be engaged in the business vision, the direction of travel, and the route map that's going to take them there. They want to be able to celebrate milestones, achievements big and small, and then, when the tough times come, they want everyone to see the fight as theirs, to work together to turn things back round.

The investment in their planning system delivers a huge return. It's a foundation system that they would not be without.

Many successful small businesses don't see planning that way.

- ▸ They view it as a pain – something you have to do for investors or the bank manager
- ▸ They feel they don't have time, preferring to 'go with the flow'

- They see it as restricting – they'd rather be flexible, able to grab opportunities as they come

- They feel they have a plan, when all they really have is a spreadsheet full of numbers

- They consider it unnecessary – why do I need to write down what's in my head?

Many small business owners are missing a trick.

But you're not going to be one of the many.

- Your team are never going to be heard asking, 'Are we there yet?'

- Your team are going to know exactly where they're going, how they're going to get there, and when they've arrived. And then you're going to celebrate – big style!

What's the point of planning?

The purpose of planning is to achieve your goal; get you to your destination; fulfil your vision of your ideal future.

That means you need to know where you're going, and why. It means you need to be clear about your destination, so you can draw up the map to get you there; decide what route you're going to take; how many stages there'll be in your journey; who you're going to take with you; and when you're going to get there.

It's about goals, strategies, tasks and schedules.

Whether you're planning for your business, or your life, the next ten years, or the next hour, your key question will always remain constant:

WHAT AM I TRYING TO ACHIEVE, AND WHY?

Your business plans may be focused on selling the business, or growing it, or franchising.

Your personal plans will be focused on your *true priorities* – those things that are *really* important to you – the creation of your ideal future.

Your plans for your team will be about their personal development, growth and contribution.

'But doesn't planning remove spontaneity and inhibit creativity?', I hear you ask.

'Doesn't it waste precious time that you could be using to *do* stuff?'

'Doesn't it make you dull?'

No, not at all. Far from it.

Planning is **the platform** on which your innovation and creativity can blossom and shine. And there are loads of other great benefits too.

▸ **Planning: brings individuals and teams together and breaks down silos**

All too often, specialist teams, or individuals within a business, even a small one like yours, can get lost in their own little world, and not be able to see the value that others bring to the business, or the challenges others face to get things done.

Regular planning creates the opportunity to bring people together from different areas of the business to review the way work is done from the customer's perspective and make plans based on what is best for the whole business.

▶ Planning: creates a safe environment for new and creative ideas

Meet 'That's not the way we do things round here' – first cousin to 'We tried that before, and it didn't work'.

It's this type of statement that will prevent the flow of ideas in your business, and even your best people will not put their creative heads above the parapet if they know they'll be shot down in flames.

Your planning system offers a structured way to talk openly about the challenges facing your business, and ask for new and creative solutions to overcome them.

▶ Planning: gives everyone the chance to contribute

How motivating and exciting to be part of something that is growing and achieving success thanks, in part, to your contribution.

Involve your team in your planning and you involve them in your vision for the future – you give them the opportunity to create it.

How much more engaged do you think they will be? How much more ownership do you think they will take?

▶ Planning: exposes your blind spots

We all have them. We can all be blind to our own strengths and weaknesses, to our innate prejudices, to other people's talents and the value they add; and often we need others to shine a light on our blind spots.

It's the same in business – we all see things from our own view point, and benefit enormously from understanding how others see things. Planning gives us a framework for this.

▶ Planning: puts the customer first

Life planning puts you first. Business planning puts the customer first, and ensures that the focus is on what's best for the customer, building trust and ensuring that everyone is focused on what really matters.

▶ Planning: keeps your products relevant

It's your customers who decide whether your products are relevant to them or not, and it's your planning system that will ensure that you check in with them; that you review your energy-vs-profit matrix; that you look for more innovative and effective ways to meet their needs and satisfy their wants.

▶ Planning: builds a stronger management team

Regular planning, focused on the business as a whole, brings the management team closer and helps them to see the value – skills, experience and expertise – that they each bring. It's also a great way of developing them, teaching them to focus on the end goal, and the strategies and tactics that will get you there.

▶ Planning: determines priorities

Your planning system is a key element in your continuous improvement cycle: plan – implement – review – plan. You start the exercise looking at what's possible, and by the end it's all about results.

You understand your long-term goal and you've plotted your course to get there. Together you've agreed your priorities, you've decided on your ninety-day goals, you have your action plan, you know your first step. It's simple and it's logical, and it's all about getting the right things done.

▶ Planning: builds ownership and accountability

Any effective plan assigns the who as well as the what, where, how and when. It gives everyone ownership for their own little piece of the business – their role, their goal, their action plan.

Ownership and accountability are the key differentiators between a regular team and a high performing team. Your plan will drive this.

▶ Planning: helps you to spot opportunities

A consistent planning system, and planning calendar, forces you to step off the hamster wheel once in a while and get your head up. To go from being a hamster to being a meerkat, if you like.

It gets you to review your progress to date: what's worked well, what hasn't, what lessons can be learned.

It provides space and time to think – about what you want to happen, what might get in the way, how you can get around any obstacles.

It opens you up to opportunities that you might otherwise miss.

With all these great benefits, what would stop you planning?

Well maybe you don't know how to plan, or how to plan effectively.

Maybe you're a dreamer rather than a doer – able to see the future clearly, but not recognising that you have to plot the steps to get there.

Perhaps you're completely overwhelmed by the day-to-day – reacting to the urgent/not important 'stuff' in your life, overwhelmed, buried under a sea of other people's priorities.

Of course, there are those who just can't be doing with the hassle of planning, and would rather just get on and *do.*

Well, sometimes in life you need to slow down to go faster. And even if you don't create detailed goals and action plans, there's a huge amount of power in spending time working out exactly what you want and then focusing on the outcome you want to achieve.

> ## SOMETIMES IN LIFE YOU NEED TO SLOW DOWN, TO GO FASTER

Life first, business second

If you're going on a long journey in your car, what do you do?

You think about where you are now, what your starting point is. You think about where you want to get to – your destination. You think about when you want to get there, maybe when you *need* to get there. And then you plan your route.

You work out which way you'll go. You plan where you want to break the journey, for a coffee or to fill up. For longer trips, you may build in a stopover. You'll know how long the journey will take, with and without traffic, and you'll be prepared for things not to go to plan. Things often don't after all.

You do all this planning for a pretty straightforward car journey. Why would you not put the same effort into planning your business journey? If you want to scale, grow or sell your business, you need to plan. And it all has to start with you, and what you want for your life!

Personal Planning

To be honest, we didn't do much personal planning at Macs. Yes, we talked about personal development, and how we could become better at our role within the business, or progress to the next level.

What we wanted out of life; what we saw as our ideal future – not so much!

Maybe we were all too young, too focused on progression, to recognise that you only get one crack at this business called life, or that, if you plan for it, you can have both – a happy, successful life and a successful business.

I get why people say they don't want to plan their life. I worked with someone once who had her whole life mapped out – she was going to be a Restaurant Manager by twenty-two, married by twenty-five, have her first child by twenty-seven, that sort of thing – and she stuck to it, right up to the point that life got in the way, and the wheels came off her perfect plan.

With any plan, you have to recognise that things happen, things change, and that every successful plan needs to be adjusted and tweaked when the opportunities, or the challenges, come.

But there are three essentials to the sort of planning that will make a real difference to your life.

1. Knowing what's *really* important to you – what your *true priorities* are (those things that would still be important if you heard the world was going to end in five years!) – the *values* you want to live by, which will govern your behaviour.

2. Being clear about what success with these true priorities looks like to you – your ideal future.

3. Having a personal management system that keeps your life and your business goals in harmony.

We'll come back to your personal management system, but for now, answer these crucial questions:

What are my True Priorities (those things that would still be important even if I knew the world was going to end in 5 years), and why are they important?

1. _____

   Why? _____

2. _____

   Why? _____

3. _____

   Why? _____

4. _____

   Why? _____

5. _____

   Why? _____

What are the Values I want to live by? _____

_____

_____

When I am successful I will be _

_ _

_ _

When I am successful I will (be doing) _

_ _

_ _

_ _

When I am successful I will have _

_ _

_ _

Know your starting point

Before you can move forward towards time and financial freedom, you need first to take a step back, and take the time to think about

- ▸ Where you are now

- ▸ Where you want to be, and

- ▸ What's blocking your path

Where are you now?

If you want to lose weight, you start by getting on the scales.

Before you can decide where you want to be and how you're going to get there, you need to be clear about where you are now – like getting on the scales, you need a baseline, a marker, to measure later success against.

Compare your life to your ideal:

- ▸ Are you happy with the hours you are working?

- ▸ Do you regularly miss family events?

▸ Do you take regular holidays?

▸ Are you able to switch off from the business?

▸ Do you regularly feel overwhelmed and anxious?

Think about how you're feeling right now, what you love about the way things are at the moment and what you want to change.

Where do you want to be?

What does success look like to you?

It's so easy to get bogged down in other people's view of success, and overwhelmed with other people's priorities; chasing other people's goals.

A successful life is way more than just a successful business or career, and yet sometimes we chase business success, at the cost of everything else.

So, what does success look like to you?

What would have to be in place? What would you be doing? Who would you be with? Where would you be? – for you to consider your life to be a success?

Do you really want that million-pound business? Maybe you do. Maybe you want a ten-million-pound business, or maybe a six-figure business would suit you just fine.

Maybe you're more about having time to be with your kids while they're growing up; with your parents while you still have them; seeing the world with your other half?

Think of those things that are really important to you; the things you would want to be remembered for; the things that would say to you, that your life was a success.

Where am I now?

Where do I want to be?

What's getting in the way/blocking my path?

Take the time to really think this through.

Why?

Because when you're really clear about what success looks like to you, then you know with absolute certainty what your *true priorities* are, and what you should be planning for.

You won't just know what you should be doing every day, but also WHY you're doing it; and you'll focus on building a business to support this ideal life, rather than building your life around your business.

What's blocking your path?

What is getting in the way of you achieving the success you're after?

Is it other people's priorities?

Is it your obsession with shiny new programmes and other people's success?

Or is it simply that you never really took the time to work out what success looks like to you, and so you've never created the plan necessary to achieve it?

Get really clear about your answers to these questions, but remember that even when you think you're crystal clear about where you are and what's blocking you, it's still only your view!

NOW   OBSTACLE   WHERE

Talk to your family and close friends

For any business owner or entrepreneur looking to build a life and not just a business, it's important to recognise the influence that your family, in particular, should have on your planning, and the impact that your business plans will have on your relationship with them – for better or worse.

Unless you are a strange and solitary fish, to some extent you will have relied on your family and close friends for emotional, maybe also financial support, as you built your business. We've all been there.

Then, with success come choices, and not always easy ones – do I invest in that piece of equipment or software or employee that will free up my time in the long-term, or do I invest in my family and their needs – private schooling, a family car, a family holiday?

How many hours will I work to grow the business, and how many will I devote to building and maintaining my close relationships? What am I prepared to make sacrosanct to build a life, even if it may mean working less, or maybe even slowing down my business growth?

How can I plan to have both great relationships and a great business? What would I need to do to never work a weekend again? What would need to be in place?

Talk to those important to you and work this out.

Just like when you want to lose weight, knowing your starting point, and being clear about your target, is essential to a successful outcome. So don't skip over this part of your planning. If you want to build a successful life, you need to be clear what that looks like.

Only when you've got this nailed will you focus in on building a business that will support the life you're aiming for.

▸ KNOW WHERE YOU'RE GOING THEN PLAN YOUR ROUTE ◂

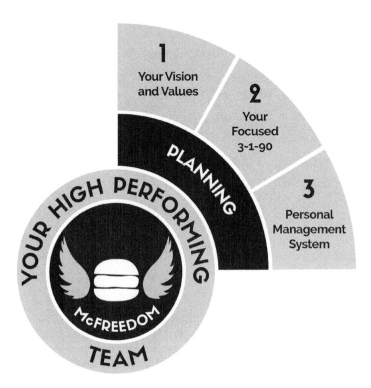

How to develop your business plan

1. Your Vision and Values

*'I have come up with a plan so cunning you could
stick a tail on it and call it a weasel.'*
BLACKADDER

Business Planning

Just like your personal planning, your business planning needs
to start with a good hard look at where you are now, where
you want to get to, and what's blocking your path.

Where are you now?

Again, just like your personal planning, your review starts with
your opinion of where you're at, and then factors in the views
of your team, your customers, and maybe even your suppliers.

You want the clearest picture possible of your starting point.

Your view

Compare your business to McDonald's:

- ▸ Are you consistent and reliable, no matter what day, or
  time of day, no matter who the customer talks to in
  your business?

- ▸ Are you available? Is it easy for your customers to find you?

- ▸ Do you have systems, and if so are they simple, logical
  and repeatable?

- ▸ How many times would you need to ask 'why?' before you uncovered the real reason you do things the way you do?

- ▸ Can you leave your team to get on and run the business for you, when you're not there?

- ▸ Are you confident that those who do work for you will do it correctly, and to the standard you expect?

Look at your business from every angle to get a really clear picture of what works and what doesn't, what you're really good at, and where you need to improve.

Your customers' view

Find out what your customers think not just about what you do for them, but also how you do it.

Check whether you satisfy the five basic expectations of every customer, that I talk about in *Process to Profit*, and which form the core of McDonald's service model.

1. Speed – do they get what they want from you when they want it?

2. A painless interaction – is your business 'friction-free' and easy to do business with?

3. Friendliness and respect – are you and your business friendly and approachable?

4. Availability – are you somewhere where your customers can find you easily? Available when they need you to be?

5. Value for money – do you deliver on their core expectations – and then some?

Ask them if you meet their needs; if you resolve their pain; if you give them a great experience. Find out what works and what doesn't; if there's anything you can do to make their lives easier. Call them, survey them, do whatever you want to do – but get that information.

Your team's view

Whether they are directly employed by you or not, anyone who does work for you is part of your team, and you need to know their views about what works and what doesn't in your business.

- ▸ Are you making their lives easier or unnecessarily complicated?

- ▸ Do you put blocks in the way of them delivering a great customer experience?

- ▸ Do they have systems to follow, or is everything a bit random and reactive?

By asking your team for their input at this stage – and listening to it – you begin to build the trust and engagement you will need when you come to install your new systems further down the line.

Think about your products

As part of your research, and in light of your customer feedback, assess your existing products and services. Are they still relevant to your customers? How could they be improved/ updated to better meet your customers' needs? How much does each product contribute to your business? Where does each sit on the energy vs profit grid?

Dig into your numbers

You will know what numbers are important to your business better than I will, but having a good handle on the following figures is a great starting point.

- ▸ What was your turnover in the last twelve months?
- ▸ What was your profitability?
- ▸ How many regular customers do you have?
- ▸ What services do these customers use?
- ▸ How many customers have you lost?
- ▸ Why did you lose them?

Get a really firm handle on where you are now, and when you have that, we'll start looking at where you want to get to.

Where do you want to get to?

When I was starting out on my own I had a dream of what I wanted to achieve, but like many dreams, it was hazy and unfocused, and I could never tell anyone what it was all about with any clarity. I wasn't absolutely clear where I was going, and we all know what happens when you're not sure where you're going... you get lost!

And I did.

I ventured down so many rabbit holes, wandered into so many blind alleys, found myself in so many cul-de-sacs, desperately trying to get to – where?

You could say it was all part of my vertical learning curve, but looking back it feels like eighteen months of wasted time, effort, and money!

Knowing your destination is crucial. It keeps you focused.

It inspires your team. It gives purpose and meaning to your planning.

What is your vision?

When you're thinking about your vision, think about the impact you want to make, the influence you want to have, the legacy you want to leave.

Think, 'the best we can be'. Think 'making a real difference'. Think big!

Your vision should give you goose bumps every time you look at it, and connect with the hearts and minds not only of your team, but also of your ideal clients.

This is about the future you see for yourself and your business, your destination, so write it in terms of the future: 'We will be... ' or 'Our vision is to be... '

AT MPL (MARIANNE PAGE LTD)

Our Vision is to be bigger than Gerber! The go-to business for six- and seven-figure business owners who want to work ON their business, not IN it; influencing every entrepreneur across the globe to build the systems that will free them to scale, sell or franchise their business... or run it from a beach somewhere.

It's not about where you are now, it's where you're headed – your destination.

What's the time frame?

People often talk about their ten-year vision for their business, and it's a great timeframe for the majority of us. But if your personal plan is to sell up and move to Bali in four years' time, then the ten-year vision doesn't really work for you.

Whatever timeframe you choose, be clear about it. Write it in a journal or pin it on your notice board as the date you're working towards. You'll need it for your planning.

Who is the vision for?

It's for you, to keep you focused, motivated, and on track.

It's for your team, to inspire them with your clarity, and engage them in the journey.

It's for your ideal clients, because it makes clear who you want to serve, and how you plan to serve them.

Don't keep your vision to yourself. Once you're happy with it, share it with the team, get their input, get them excited about it, and then get it out there on your website, your marketing materials, your training resources.

This is a big deal. Putting it out there is the first step towards achievement, so take it now.

My Vision

Next, your values.

What are values?

The dictionary defines values as, 'Principles or standards of behaviour; one's judgement of what is important in life.'

For me, they are your compass; they're about the way you choose to live your life and run your business. In owner-run businesses, the two are inextricably linked.

We all have values whether we recognise them as such, or not, and our life is much easier when we understand what they are and align our plans, decisions and behaviours with them.

For example, if you value family, but you work seventy-hour weeks, you'll feel internal stress and conflict. If you don't value financial risk, you're unlikely to start your own business.

Being clear about your values helps you to make decisions and take actions that are fully aligned with them. When you're in tune with your values, your gut will reflect them. Go against your gut and you might well be going against your values.

As you move through life, your values may change. For example, when you start out, success – measured by money and status – might be a top priority. But as you get older, perhaps after you have a family, you may value work-life harmony more.

Keeping in touch with your values is a lifelong exercise.

When thinking about what your values are, ask yourself:

- How do I want my business, and the people in it, to operate?

- What are the principles I hold dear, that I won't compromise, that I would like my business to be known for?

- What are the qualities I aspire to – that I live my life by, and want my team to share?

- How do I want to run my business?

Decide what's important to you and how you'll demonstrate it in your business, because what you do is a megaphone for what you believe in.

You may genuinely believe and therefore say, one thing, but your actions and behaviours may well be saying another.

Let me give you an example from a private client I worked with last year, and the feedback I gave them in a report on their business, which illustrates the point.

'You say that you want a quality operation, but your team believe that you won't pay enough to bring in quality people.'

'You say that you want a team that takes ownership for their role and how it is performed, but your team see you needing to be consulted on every decision, and keeping tight control.'

'You say that you want a fast-paced organisation that grows at speed, but you over-analyse everything and take forever to make decisions.'

'You make commitments – to have management team meetings, to bring in a structured bonus scheme and so on – but don't stick to these commitments.'

'You say that you value your people – but your contracted working hours, holidays, and pay structure is sending a different message to the team, who also see you working very long hours.'

'You say that you value your clients and want them to have first class service – but you appear 'laid back' about, and accepting of, failure to deliver on time.'

WHAT YOU DO IS A MEGAPHONE FOR WHAT YOU BELIEVE IN.

So what do you believe in? What would your team say you value?

At this point, business owners will usually say things like honesty, integrity, customer focus, maybe fairness – clearly good values, but to be honest, these are standard principles that every business owner should live by. Business values 101. The expected minimum.

Your values are all about you and the personality of your business; you're going to hire team members who share those values; you're going to attract customers who love your values; you want these values to inspire, to attract, to hold everything together.

A brand strategy business I know has the following as their values:

- Build inspiration
- Dream bigger
- Embrace quirky
- Tell it like it is
- Expand your world
- Live the brand

That's who they are. That's how they behave. Everything about their brand fits with these values.

The business values that will define who we are, and make our business special are

_____

_____

_____

_____

_____

_____

_____

Who are you?

Honesty and integrity are a given – there's so much more to your business than that – so let's get creative, let's get the team involved, and let's work out what makes you and your business special.

Values and your business culture

People often get confused between business values and business culture. A good way to think of it is:

Values are what you begin with; culture is what you end with.

For example, 'Tell it like it is' may be a core value to you and your business, but if enough people in your business just tell the customer what they want to hear, or shy away from tough decisions, then eventually your business will be known for playing it safe.

Your business culture develops through the actions of the people within it.

The only way to control these actions is through ongoing communication, through appreciative and constructive feedback that reinforces your values, and, most importantly – through your personal example.

Action and behaviour drive culture more than words ever will.

So, to build a business culture aligned to your values you must define, communicate, and consistently reinforce your values.

2. Your Focused 3-1-90

'Lack of direction, not lack of time, is the problem. We all have twenty-four-hour days.'
ZIG ZIGLAR

How are you going to achieve your vision?

Focus is the key!

Even with a clear vision, it's easy to get overwhelmed by the mountain of ideas, tactics and goals that might lead us towards its achievement. So we need a way to chunk the mountain down into smaller more manageable hills.

I call these smaller hills my Focus Areas!

Focus Areas

The corporates may look on them as strategies, some may think of them simply as priorities. The name doesn't really matter. What does matter is that you have them – that you take your mountain, look at what it's made up of, and group similar goals, ideas and tactics together.

Remember though, this is all about focus, so you can't have a dozen focus areas – it kind of defeats the object of the exercise. Four or five, maximum six, will keep you properly focused and make your planning and delivery a whole lot easier.

For example, McDonald's focus on People, Place, Promotion, Price, Product.

At MPL (Marianne Page Ltd) we also have five areas for focus: Bums on Seats, Visibility & Influence, Products, Partnerships and People.

For each focus area we set an overall aim, or intention, that's in line with our vision, and which will move us closer to achieving it. As you read our intentions for each focus area take note of the language – it's 'act as if' language - we say that it is as we want it to be, then it's up to each member of the team to make what we say we do, a reality.

Bums on Seats

- ▸ We attract the business owners who will benefit most from The McFreedom System®

- ▸ We stay true to our limited numbers principle, to enable us to give focused attention to every business owner who works with us

- ▸ We fill the room with six- and seven-figure business owners for every McFreedom Secrets workshop

Visibility & Influence

- ▸ The Marianne Page brand is recognised as the go-to for six- and seven-figure business owners who want to scale, grow, sell or franchise

- We have a reputation for quality, service and delivery on our promises
- We are regularly invited to speak at events, and comment in the media, aimed at successful business owners

Products

- We develop and deliver world class products which move our clients closer to their McFreedom
- We serve a global market

Partnerships

- We develop mutually beneficial relationships with partner businesses, who can add value to our clients, or where we can add value to theirs

People

- We have a high performing core team, plus a number of trusted associates, who deliver a world-class service to our clients, both online and offline

People is an essential focus area for every business, guiding hiring and development decisions, ensuring that you have the right people, in the right place, at the right time to move the business forward. Your people plan will underpin and support your other focus areas.

So, these are the focus areas and intentions that I believe will take us to **our** vision. What are yours?

Focus Area _
Intention _
_ _
_ _

Focus Area _
Intention _
_ _
_ _

Focus Area _
Intention _
_ _
_ _

Focus Area _
Intention _
_ _
_ _

Focus Area _
Intention _
_ _
_ _

When you are clear what your focus areas are, and what you want each focus area to deliver for you – your aim or intention – you can then begin to develop fully focused goals and plans.

3-1-90 Planning

Your planning system is in fact, a *planning cycle* where you will plan, do, review over and over again at planned (naturally) intervals. In The McFreedom System® we talk about 3-1-90 planning.

Why 3-1-90?

For me, three years is the ideal timeframe for long-term planning – long enough to keep you driving forward, and short enough to recognise the outcomes you're achieving and adjust course if you need to.

You then have your more detailed plan for the coming financial year and, at regular ninety-day intervals, you assess, adjust and set goals for the next ninety days.

So, a three-year (3) high level plan, then a more detailed plan for the first year (1), with progress reviewed every ninety days (90): 3-1-90.

What you're plotting is your route map – the journey, in stages, that you and your team are going to take to reach your destination.

At every stage of your planning, from mapping out the next three years, to planning the next day, you'll refer back to your vision by asking yourself the key question:

WHAT AM I TRYING TO ACHIEVE, AND WHY?

Everything is built on the answer to this question – focus areas, goals, targets, deadlines, milestones, measures of success – all the essential elements in an effective plan.

Developing your 3-year plan

Now that you're clear about your vision (and the date you've written down for its achievement), ask yourself:

'If I'm going to achieve my vision by [then], what needs to be in place by the end of my third financial year? What do I need to have achieved by then in each of my focus areas?'

Then for each focus area, decide what the goal or goals will be.

The People Plan

When you're developing your people plan you need key information to hand:

1. What you're going to deliver in each focus area in the next three years; the goals that you've just developed.

2. The strengths, weaknesses and potential of your existing team.

3. The gaps that you would need to fill through training or recruitment, in order to have the right people, with the right skills in place when you need them.

Our Vision (Toe-tingling, goosebump-giving, inspirational vision)			
SMART Goals 3 Year Overview		From _____ Until _____	
Focus Area + Aims	Goal	Outcome	
SERVICE We set the bar for the standard of service for the widget-making industry - this is referred to as the ABC standard	To achieve and launch the ABC standard of service excellence by (date 3 years from now)		
PEOPLE To employ individuals who buy into the ABC culture of excellence and develop them to reach their full potential as team members and people	To employ and develop (and pass probation) the team in line with the 3 year vision organisational chart by (date 3 years from now)		
INFRASTRUCTURE To create an environment and provide the resources whereby people can reach their full potential			
GROWTH To have trebled in turnover			

In developing your people plan you'll be focused on the big question, 'What am I trying to achieve, and why?', and any hiring that you do will then be focused on, and a requirement for, the achievement of one or more of your 3-year goals.

You'll have identified a gap in your team, determined that you have no one in the team who either has the right skills now – or can be developed into the role – and made a strategic decision to hire someone new.

You'll ask questions like:

▸ What new jobs will need to be filled?

▸ What new skills will be needed?

▸ Is there anyone in the team who has those skills or who could be trained?

▸ Are we making the most of individual team members' strengths and abilities?

▸ Do we need to hire a new manager, or is there someone in the team who has leadership skills?

Then, based on the answers to these questions, you'll make a plan for the role you want to fill, the type of person you're going to be looking for, and the timing of the activities necessary to get them in place at the time you need them.

Annual Planning – your next financial year

Once you have your 3-year goals, and people plan, start thinking about your next financial year.

Ask yourself: 'Ok, if I want to be *there* by [insert date for end of your third financial year], what needs to be in place by the end of *this* financial year? What do I need to have achieved by then in each of my focus areas?'

While your 3-year goals can be broad and unassigned, your 1-year goals must be SMART, and for me that means:

- ▸ Specific – A specific goal is clear and distinct. It defines as much of the goal as possible

- ▸ Measurable – What gets measured gets done. A measure gives feedback and lets you know when the goal has been completed

- ▸ Assigned – A goal must be assigned to an individual or a team

- ▸ Realistic – A realistic goal is challenging, but achievable within the timeframe

- ▸ Time-bound – Timeframes must be challenging but realistic

Each goal must be focused on the aim of the focus area it sits under *and* move you closer to your big vision.

Make each goal as SMART as possible – dates, times, names, amounts.

Take a break

Just as you would on any long journey, you need to take regular breaks to re-energise and re-focus so when you're pulling your 1-year plan together, don't forget to plan *and book* your holidays.

In fact, make it a priority. Not only do holidays act as a great deadline to work towards, but they're also an essential re-energiser for your mind, body and spirit.

If you're going to deliver on these challenging plans you're developing, you're going to need regular quality breaks, and besides, you're building a life, not just a business. Remember?

Your 90-day goals

So why the 90-day timeframe?

I read a great blog once which talked about the 90-day timeframe as, 'The range where ambition and planning actually fall reasonably close together'.

And it's true. We all have a really good feel for what we can get done in ninety days – how far we can move towards a big goal – and plan the steps that we need to take to get there.

Our longer-term plans, even though it's valuable to have them, can't be planned right down to concrete steps; the goals are too big, there's too much to get done, and if we try to plan the detail we just get overwhelmed, which in turn leads to inaction.

Working with 90-day goals keeps us moving forward, keeps us agile and on our toes; able to tackle challenges and grab opportunities as they come along; adjusting our plans for the *next* ninety days to accommodate them.

So, when you have your 1-year plan, break it down into 90-day chunks, with goals that you'll decide on by asking:

'Ok, so if I want to be *there* by the end of this financial year [insert date], where do I need to be in the next ninety days [insert date]?'

3-1-90 Example - Peter's Perfect Pasties
FOCUS AREAS People Products Visibility Location
THE PERFECT PIE VISION To be the number one supplier of cheese & onion pasties to high end delicatessens in northern Europe
3 YEAR GOAL Establish a network of sales people across northern Europe, supplying Perfect Pies to 5 different countries
1 YEAR GOAL Have 4 UK sales managers in place by the end of this financial year
90 DAY GOAL Recruit a sourcing manager with experience in pie and pasty distribution

Do this for each focus area, and each big goal for the coming year, and repeat every 90 days, involving the team as much as you can.

The 3-1-90 planning system is a great way to keep momentum and deliver continuous improvement, but as with many things in your business, it needs to become a routine, and then a habit, in order to deliver its full effect.

As your business grows, your planning system becomes increasingly important, and potentially more time-consuming, so it's vital that you allocate time for it to ensure that it gets done.

> **IT'S A CYCLE, AND YOU HAVE TO KEEP PEDALLING!**

3. Your Personal Management System

*'I went to a bookstore and asked the saleswoman,
"Where's the self-help section?" She said if she
told me, it would defeat the purpose.'*
GEORGE CARLIN

I've been there, and I'm sure you have too – having so much to do that you do nothing, other than stress about it? So much work piling up on your desk that you can't concentrate on the task in hand?

How often do you hear business owners say, 'There just isn't enough time in the day to get everything done that I need to'?

How often do you say it yourself? Once a week? Once a month?

How often do you get to the end of the day wondering where your time went, feeling frustrated that you didn't achieve what you set out to? Or miss deadlines that you set yourself, to launch a product, write a chapter of your book, update your website?

How many times have you let friends or your family down because you were 'just too busy' to stick to plans you'd made to spend time with them?

It's a common problem, and a big cause of stress for many business owners, so you're certainly not alone!

But it doesn't have to be.

Let me ask you a different question: How often do you hear the most successful business people complaining about a lack of time, or being too busy? How often do you think they miss deadlines, or break commitments?

So, what's the difference between them and you? How can they run multi-million pound operations, take several holidays a year, and find time for new projects and products, without breaking sweat, let alone feeling any stress?

Simple!

They have a strategy – a personal system for managing their time and their workload. Something that they have developed through trial and error, and refined as their business, and commitments, have grown.

While you are bumbling along with a half-baked set of unspecific, anything but SMART goals, and a jumbled list of things 'to do', they are following their carefully structured plans, sticking religiously to their daily disciplines, and celebrating the achievement of their milestones.

Time is money, and the most successful business owners don't waste a penny of it.

I have my own strategy for productivity. Bits of it are a takeaway from my time at McDonald's, bits I learned from modelling successful business owners, and some bits I've developed over time, based on what works for me and what doesn't.

There are a number of elements to it, but in a nutshell it consists of three things:

1. Knowing the answer to the question, 'What am I trying to achieve, and why?'

2. Planning and scheduling everything

3. Sticking to a set of daily routines and success habits

With your 3-1-90 plans in place, you need a strategy that maximises your personal productivity and delivers on those plans, one day at a time.

Dealing with Overwhelm

First things first – let's sort this thing called overwhelm.

Over the past few years I've talked to a lot of business owners who are struggling with how much they have to get done, and let's face it, us business owners have a *lot* of 'stuff' to do.

So much stuff and all of it urgent. A bulging inbox controlling our day, forcing us to react, impossible to prioritise.

Just overwhelming!

Of course, everyone has days like this – where you can't see the wood for the trees, where your to-do list for the day is so long it will take you to the middle of next week just to get through half of it.

Those days when you don't feel like your life is your own; when you're working to other people's priorities and everyone wants a piece of you; when you feel completely chaotic and out of control.

As one-offs, these days are manageable – there are simple tools and techniques to get you through them, to deal with them, and still get stuff done. But it's when these days start to merge, when as a new client said to me, 'Overwhelm becomes the norm', when you forget where the hell you're going, let alone how you're going to get there.

That's when overwhelm has become a real issue.

That's when you lose focus on your vision; when what's really important to you seems a million miles away.

So what do you do? You go chasing off down rabbit holes looking for the answers – in time-management programmes and apps.

You start subscribing to lots of 'successful people' – you know, those people who seem to have it all – looking for the magic pill that's going to bring you their success. And of course, that's exactly what it is – *their* success.

You start to believe that success only comes through long hours and even harder work.

You lose sight of what's really important to you; what success means to you; what your ideal future looks like.

So, what can you do about it?

Well, you can build your personal management system around one killer question.

What am I trying to achieve, and why?

I'm a pretty organised person these days, and this one question (ok, technically two) still has a massive impact on how focused

I am, and how much I get done on a day-to-day and month-to-month basis.

It's a powerful question, whether you're thinking about the next three years, or the next three hours.

To find your answer, go back to what we talked about in part one when we looked at your personal vision – what you really want for yourself – the *big dream*.

Are you really clear about what you're trying to achieve, and why? Because when you are, you're ready for the exercise that will get rid of overwhelm every time it raises its ugly head.

And here it is:

1. Decide on the timeframe that's overwhelming you. Is it what you have on today, tomorrow, the coming week, the coming month?

2. Next, get yourself a big sheet of paper and a pen.

3. Write down everything – and I mean *everything* you believe you have to get done in the coming week: personal, business, everything...

4. Once you've done that – once you've exhausted everything – and you're sure you have it all on that sheet of paper, grab a big, black marker pen.

5. Go through your list and cross off everything that doesn't move you towards what you're trying to achieve; everything that doesn't move you towards your big vision.

    Be ruthless here, look for other people's priorities on this list and get them crossed off. Look for things that are easy to do, or that feed your inner procrastinator – like setting up a to-do list app, or reading through all those emails you've subscribed to – and get those crossed off too.

Cross off anything that doesn't move you to where you now know that you want to be. Ruthless is the key word.

6. There will be things on your list that do have to be done, but most of them should *not* be done by you; things like book-keeping, expenses, managing your database.

   These things can stay, but they get moved onto a second list, called 'Delegate'. Add all the things that need to be done, but not by you, to this list

   Recognise those things that you may be busying yourself with that are not moving you, or your business, or your life in the right direction.

What you are left with after this exercise are three lists:

▸ Your Do list – the things you're going to do because they move you towards your Vision

- ▸ Your Delegate list – things that you're going to get other people to do
- ▸ Your Ditch list – full of other people's stuff, and things that you've just got into the bad habit of adding to your list every day

DO, DITCH OR DELEGATE!

When we get to Foundation #3 we'll talk about who to delegate to and how to delegate effectively, but for now, just give this a go and see what it does for your overwhelm. I promise you, it works like magic.

You have to be ruthless, though, and you have to get over your guilt about ditching other people's priorities. Just remember that's exactly what they are – other people's priorities, not yours! You have plenty of your own to be getting on with.

Developing Success Habits

Did you know that around 95% of everything you think, feel, do and achieve is the result of habit?

So the habits that are making you productive or unproductive, keeping you stuck or making you successful, right now, have almost certainly been with you since your youth.

Unsuccessful people have a number of common habits – habits that revolve around the words 'should', 'must' and 'have to'; habits that feed their inner procrastinator; habits that keep them stuck.

Successful people have habits in common too – habits that keep them focused, keep them prosperous, keep them making great decisions and enjoying life.

And the great news? New habits can be learned.

You can develop new patterns of behaviour by modelling the habits of successful people and making them part of your personal management system.

Success habits like:

► Setting daily goals

► Reading/listening to a business book a month

► Getting up before 7:00am

► Exercising for thirty minutes every day

► Giving back/contributing

► Practising focus on one thing at a time

► Having a date-night/friends-night once a week/month

Even better news – there's a proven **seven-step formula** for embedding a new habit into your psyche:

► Step 1   Decide what habit you want to install

► Step 2   Tell people what you're doing – make it public

► Step 3   For at least twenty-one days, stick religiously to the habit – no exceptions, no excuses

► Step 4   Act as if – visualise yourself doing it – use the power of muscle memory

► Step 5   Develop an affirmation you repeat over and over. 'I get up and get going immediately at 6:00am', 'I arrive five minutes early for everything'

► Step 6   Show resolve and commitment – persist until it's second nature – a hard habit to break

► Step 7   Reward yourself to reinforce and reaffirm

The Henry Habit

Take Henry, for example. Henry was tasked by his school to read more, and challenged by his dad Peter, to read for thirty minutes every day.

So that was Step 1 – Henry was to read for thirty minutes a day. Both Henry and his dad told friends and me about the challenge (Step 2) and then for one month, every single day, Henry would announce both when his half hour started, when it had finished, and how many pages he'd read (Step 3).

With this habit, Henry had to act as if he was enjoying it, to talk about it as something he looked forward to every day (Steps 4 and 5).

He stayed the course, completed his month, and was suitably rewarded for his perseverance (Steps 6 and 7).

Did the habit stick?

Of course not – he's a thirteen-year-old boy! But, as a result of supporting Henry in his habit-forming activity, his dad has developed The Henry Habit, and now reads one business book a month, in thirty minutes every day!

This formula really does work. Give it a try!

Your Daily Routine – habits to maximise your productivity

Your daily routine is the cornerstone of your personal management system, and should be crammed full of habits that will maximise your productivity, and move you closer to your big vision.

Get into the habit of planning your day the evening before (and your week on a Sunday evening). At the end of the day you're usually very clear about what still needs to done, what the priorities are, what tomorrow's priority will be. Advanced planning like this makes sure that you hit the ground running.

Chunk your work into ninety-minute segments. This is a good timeframe for focus, and *focus* is the key word – don't multi-task – if you're going to work on a sales letter, work on it for the full ninety minutes, or until it's done, if you can do it quicker.

Work out which part of the day you're at your peak – for me it's first thing in the morning – and use that ninety minutes to 'eat your frog' – i.e. do the thing that you don't necessarily want to do, but that's weighing you down mentally, because you know you really need to get it done.

Just get focused and eat the damn frog! It's a really good success habit to get into.

Set yourself mini deadlines – always good for those of us who like a bit of 'last minute pressure' – make them 'drop-dead' lines too! Absolute must delivers!

Breaks are always a good deadline. Holidays are also excellent. Ever noticed how much more you get done in the days leading up to a holiday, or the minutes leading up to any deadline. Both breaks and holidays are essential for your long-term productivity too – refreshing and re-energising your mind and body. The most successful businessmen and women really get this and have made breaks, long and short, a habit they will always keep.

Other daily routines and success habits that are good for your mind and body include taking at least thirty minutes exercise a day – even if it's just a walk down the road and back – and drinking plenty of water – two litres is the recommended amount, isn't it? I'm no scientist, but I can testify to the power of a lunchtime walk for clearing your head and setting you up for a productive afternoon.

For successful business owners there are two other personal management essentials:

1. An assistant

There are only so many things that you can be brilliant at, or that really get your juices flowing; for everything else, you need an assistant – someone who will keep you organised, and do the really important, but really boring (to you) stuff that eats away at your time.

If you're still booking your own travel, organising meeting rooms, doing your own book-keeping, maintaining your own website, managing your own CRM, then stop! And hire an assistant.

A mentor of mine refers to the £10ph, £100ph and £1,000ph tasks in your business. Which are you spending all of your precious time on?

And talking of mentors, the second essential is:

2. A mentor

How many times would you have to get lost trekking in The Himalayas – how much time and effort would you expend – before you hired a guide?

For me it was once – my partner Sas and I walked five hours up and down steep hills in the wrong direction and had to walk five hours back to where we'd started, laden down with heavy rucksacks, losing a whole day in the process, before we realised the error of our ways and hired a guide – who also carried our rucksacks into the bargain!

When you're trying to lose weight – when you really want to – do you go it alone, or do you hire a personal trainer or join a slimming club? I joined a club and followed the plan and not only lost the weight, but learned the strategies to keep it off.

Who do you trust when you're going somewhere you've never been before – your own instincts for direction, or the satnav that knows the fastest route?

Why did Andy Murray hire Ivan Lendl? To push him and guide him and develop a plan that would make him first Wimbledon Champion and then World Number 1.

How far would Luke Skywalker have got without the mentoring of Yoda?

What I've learned from the mentors I've worked with is that they get you to the next level faster; they get you to raise your game – to see things from a different viewpoint; they share their expertise to help you grow.

They're objective: they're not attached to the wallpaper of your life like you are. They stop you wasting time and money and keep you focused and away from distractions. They hold you accountable and push you to deliver results faster. They give you their simple, proven strategies and help you to develop plans that work effectively.

Your mentor is a key member of your support team – the sounding board and advisor who speeds up your journey to the results you're looking for.

A final thought about personal management

It's very easy to get stuck in a rut. Sometimes we don't even recognise that we're in one. A rut's boring, same old, same old. Dull, right? And that's not our life!

Well what if it is?

Many successful small business owners get stuck in a rut. It's called The Struggle, and while it's anything but boring, it's definitely a rut. Some find that they can't get out of it. Many more don't want to. It's comfortable, they know where they're at with it, it's their norm.

They tell themselves that they've already stepped out of their comfort zone to create their business. They tell themselves that they are successful, and that running a successful business comes at a price – no time and no life beyond it. They tell themselves they're ok with that, and they're surrounded by other strugglers who confirm that they're right.

They revel in war stories of their eighty-hour weeks, and comfort themselves that they are still working to improve themselves by attending weekend seminars and late evening webinars, while other 'less successful' people are enjoying time with family and friends. They've created a new comfort zone, and their rut's too deep to see beyond it.

Your personal management system will get you out of your rut, but it needs three things to be successful:

1. Discipline – in developing your success habits and daily routines, in ditching the stuff that doesn't serve you and delegating to your assistant and your team, in listening to your mentor.

2. Integrity – keeping your commitments to others, and to yourself, persevering with your habits and sticking to deadlines.

3. Celebration – celebrating all of your wins, no matter how small they are.

Learn to manage yourself, and the business will be a piece of cake!

PLANNING IN PRACTICE

When I first met Tom I asked to see his vision and plans for the coming year, and he handed me a spreadsheet full of numbers.

A spreadsheet with a big number on the top and lots of little numbers below it.

I asked him what it meant, and he just said, 'Well my vision is to get to £10 million in revenue in the next ten years.'

'Well, that's more of a goal,' I said. 'What will that mean to you? What will you be, who will you be with, what will you be doing? And how exactly are you going to get there?'

'With hard work from me and the team,' was his reply.

And do you know what, I don't doubt he would have achieved his goal – just on the back of his very hard work. He'd have lost a few people on the way, and there's a chance he would have lost his relationship with his partner, which was already a bit ropey. He'd have got there, but at a big cost.

So we sat down together and talked about what his vision *really* was – what all that money was for. It turned out that he wanted to build his own house in the country, for him and his young family; have time to spend with them as they grew up; take his partner on lovely holidays; franchise his business and take it overseas. He'd worked out that £10 million was the figure that he needed to make it all possible.

With that vision in mind, we then started planning exactly how it would be achieved.

- ▸ What infrastructure he would need to have in place

- ▸ What products he would have

- ▸ How many customers would need to buy how many products

We looked at his team

- ▸ Who he'd need to have with him; what skills they'd need to have

Together we set milestones along the way that he could celebrate with the team when they achieved them.

Like planning the journey to your favourite holiday destination – planning should be focused, it should be fun, and it should involve your team. So, Tom took the plans we'd begun to an away-day with the team, where they worked on them together.

We helped the team to develop SMART goals that they all bought into.

I didn't have all the answers – but I had the questions that would get him and his team to think in the right way, and together they created a route map that they now follow – 90-day chunks at a time.

These are the sort of plans I want for you.

Take a little time now to think about what you will change or do differently in your business to improve your planning.

FOUNDATION #1 TOP 5 TAKEAWAYS

1. Your planning system is the platform on which your McFreedom will be built, giving you direction, a route map to follow, and the values you're going to live by.

2. Your vision sets the direction. Your values act as your compass - guiding your decisions, actions and behaviour.

3. Your Focused 3-1-90 is the route map that keeps you focused on your destination and driving towards it; providing the rhythm for your business.

4. Your personal management system is what keeps you on track and stops you getting distracted and overwhelmed.

5. What you *do* is a megaphone for what you believe in.

FOUNDATION #1 MY ACTIONS

Priority

1. _____

2. _____

3. _____

Do one thing

The baby step I'll take TODAY is _____

_____

_____

_____

_____

CHAPTER 3

Foundation #2 Process

As the Crow Flies

Keeping things simple for your customers and your team

How easy are you to do business with?

As part of my planning for the coming year, I always ask a couple of objective people who I don't know well to check me and the business out online. I want to know how easy we are to find, how clear our message is, how simple it is to understand what our products are, and buy them.

Their report hasn't always made good reading.

Like many business owners, I used to make the mistake of thinking that what was crystal clear and obvious to me would be crystal clear to my ideal client. That they would take the time to jump through my hoops, or click more than once, to find out more about me and my products.

Like many business owners, I'd over-complicated my very simple business, I'd given visitors to my website too much choice, I'd added bells and whistles, thinking it was a good thing.

Like many business owners, I'd made myself difficult to do business with, forgetting the lessons I'd learned at McDonald's about visibility, accessibility and simplicity.

- ▶ Visibility – make sure that you're somewhere that your ideal clients can see you. Then have great branding – your equivalent of the Golden Arches sky sign.

- ▶ Accessibility – be available when and where they need you to be, easy to reach and easy to understand.

▶ Simplicity – be easy to do business with; straightforward; no hoops, no added complications, no unnecessary steps in your process.

Bear in mind that you can't be all things to all people. McDonald's tried the salad route once, remember? And soon reverted to what they were known for, and what they do best.

Keeping things simple; making it easy for your customers and your team, is what this chapter is all about.

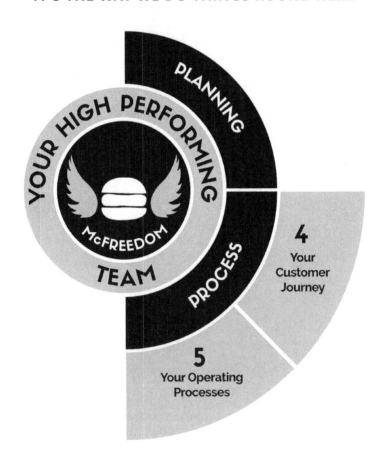

4. Your Customer Journey

*'You cannot improve one thing by 1000% but
you can improve 1000 little things by 1%.'*
JAN CARLZON

What is a customer journey?

As it sounds, the customer journey is the route your customer takes through your business from first deciding that they want what you have, to choosing to buy what they want from you, through every step of your sales process, to receiving and paying for their goods or services, and hopefully leaving you good feedback.

As a Restaurant Manager at McDonald's, I was tasked with walking my customer journey (or doing a 'Travel Path', as it was called), every hour.

This meant walking out of my restaurant, walking about 100 yards (it was definitely yards, not metres for me) up the street, or into the car park, and then walking back to the restaurant, looking for what my customers might see and notice.

▶ Was there any litter in the shrubs, or on the pavement?

▶ Was the planting looking good?

▶ Was the sign fully lit, with all the bulbs working?

▶ Was the glass on the door free of smears?

Once back inside the restaurant, I'd look for the first impression that the customer would get.

▶ Tables cleared and clean?

▶ Floor swept and mopped?

▸ Crew smart and working as they should be?

▸ No queues?

You get the picture.

Of course, we don't all have bricks and mortar businesses. For many of us that first impression is online, and very often will begin with a Google search, followed by our website, maybe followed by a phone call, and so on.

It's the same, but different.

How to map out your customer journey

Every customer goes on a journey through your business. They may take slightly different routes, they may enter and exit at different points, they may leave delighted or disappointed.

Of course, you want to give them the best possible experience, and to do that you need to understand the key phases of their journey, the Moments of Truth along the way, and any opportunities for improvement.

Whatever your customer journey is, it's important that you view it through your customer's eyes; through their very real experience.

Take off those rose-tinted specs of yours, and see the reality – not what the experience should be, or what you want it to be, but what it actually is, day-to-day.

Ask those in your team who work with the journey every day, how simple and straightforward it is; how many hoops you're making your customers jump through; how much unnecessary information you're asking your customer to provide.

An effective customer journey map gives you a clear and detailed picture of how your customer uses your product or services, and how customers and potential customers go through the buying process.

It gives you and your team an overview of your customers' experience and shows how they move through your sales funnel, which in turn helps you to identify opportunities to improve their experience.

To make it effective, you need to rethink what you believe you know, and fully understand every touch point a customer has with your business.

There's no one template that fits all businesses when it comes to mapping your customer journey, but there is a system, what a surprise!

If this is your first attempt at mapping, then the most important thing is to keep it as simple as possible, but make sure it gives you all the vital information that you need.

STEP 1
Make sure that you know
your customers – intimately

You'll have been told by lots of different gurus, mentors and experts about the importance of building your customer avatars. For customer journey mapping, these avatars are essential – giving you insights into your customers' motivations, their buying habits, what they think, how they make buying decisions, what they want to achieve and so on.

To get the best possible results, you'll create a customer journey map for each avatar.

STEP 2
Work out the phases in your customer journey

How do potential customers hear about you? What are their first interactions with you?

What is their step by step experience with you?

Your customer phases may include things like:

- Research
- Discovery
- Choice

- Purchase
- Recommend

For your first map, keep it simple and don't over-think things.

STEP 3
Know what your customers want to achieve

In customer journey mapping, it's crucial to keep in mind that this is not about *you*, it's all about *your customers*. It's all about what *they* need, what *they* want, *their* pain, *their* goals.

Go through each phase of your map and think about what your customer wants and needs when they're in this phase, so that you can give them what they are looking for.

For example, if they are looking to put a toe in the water and try your products out before they commit to a purchase, but you don't have any free resources, then you are not helping them to accomplish their goal.

Or if they are trying to find you online, but your website is not ranked on Google, then again you have stopped them from accomplishing their goal. You have put an insurmountable hurdle in their way.

List your customers' goals clearly under each of the phases in the journey map, because you can only accomplish your goals if your customers accomplish theirs.

STEP 4
Identify the touchpoints and Moments of Truth on your customer journey

For each phase, identify the interaction points between you and your customer, and the opportunities you have to connect and engage with your customers as they try to reach their goals.

These will include interactions that you have off site and onsite, through marketing, in person, and over the phone.

Some of these touchpoints are more critical than others, e.g. when they try to call you does someone answer the phone, and how do they answer the phone?

These are your Moments of Truth. Map them out too as you will need to pay particular attention to them when you come to take action.

STEP 5
Understand your time-frames

Work out the time it takes for a customer to move through each phase of their journey with you. Is there more that you could do to help your customer achieve their goal for that phase, or speed up their journey?

STEP 6
Assess the team members/external support involved in each interaction

Look at who you have involved in supporting the customer journey.

- ▸ Do you have 'aces in their places'?
- ▸ Are your best people looking after and monitoring the Moments of Truth?
- ▸ Do they have the support they need?
- ▸ Are they following simple, logical and repeatable systems to get the job done?
- ▸ Have they had enough training? The right training?

A chain is only as strong as its weakest link.

For your customers to accomplish their goals in each phase of their journey through your business, there must be effective systems in place, and well- trained people owning and running those systems.

Walk through every step of the customer journey with your team, and at each step ask 'Why?'. Why do we have this step, do we really need it, does it add value for our customers? Why do we do it this way, could we make it easier?

You want your journey to be as simple and straightforward as possible for your customers. Friction-free. Easy to do business with.

Once you have that, then you will look at how your team support it.

5. Your Operating Processes

*'If you are persistent you will get it. If you
are consistent you will keep it.'*
JEROMY SHINGONGO

It's just 'The way we do things round here'

Now this is the point where you've probably sat up, thinking
'right, better pay attention to this bit, this is the bit I need –
operating processes'.

Well you're probably right, and you're probably wrong.

I've lost track of the number of times I've been asked to, 'just
come in and do our processes – we don't need that people bit,
we've got HR'.

Yes, you're right, you do need processes to support your customer journey, but you're also wrong because you need them
for your planning: to make sure you have a clear destination
and route map to get you there; for your people to make sure
you hire the right people and train them to follow your way
of doing things; and for your performance management, to
keep everyone on track.

It's a business jigsaw that needs all four pieces to be complete.

So yes, sit up and pay attention to this bit – but do the same for the other foundations too, because you need them all.

Before we go any further, I have a confession to make – a guilty secret to let you in on – I have a problem with process!

Don't get me wrong, I love what it does, the results you can achieve through it, but the word itself chips a little piece off my soul, makes me think of bureaucracy, paperwork, jumping through hoops. My mind turns to ISO9001, Lean six sigma and the like. Things that are so not me, words that turn me off probably as much as they do you.

I lost count of the number of times I'd use the word 'process' at networking meetings, and see the shutters go down. I'd use the softer, more business-owner-friendly term 'systems' and they'd think I was a techie, into software and IT. I used language that put me in a box that no-one wanted to open 'except in emergency'!

You know what I mean. You're a 'get on and do it' person, and the people who love process are the 'Rule-Bound Reggies' of this world, paralysed by the need to analyse, lacking creativity, shackled by the need to 'follow the system' – right?

Well, sometimes!

The truth is, we all need to get past the language.

For years, I labelled myself as a process person, even called my first book *Process to Profit*, when really I'm a 'making life easier' person.

The only reason a process or a system exists is to make life easier for you, your managers, your team, your customers.

There is no other reason for them.

At McDonald's there is a system for everything, from toasting buns to taking on a new supplier; from mopping the floor to assessing franchisee performance. Yet I don't remember ever really talking about having systems. They weren't something we did in addition to the day job, they weren't viewed as hard work, or an added complication. We worked with them every single day, unconsciously. It was just the way things got done. I'm sure it still is.

And that's what I want for you and your business.

The way we do things round here

I want you to stop thinking about Process; I want you to stop fretting about developing systems; and I want you to focus on making 'the way we do things round here'

SIMPLE   LOGICAL   REPEATABLE

Looking back at the way we did things at Macs, these were the three key ingredients of each and every system that are imprinted on my mind.

Three words that encapsulate why McDonald's systems work.

- ▸ **Simple** – as simple as possible, but no simpler
- ▸ **Logical** – to a third party because what seems logical and necessary to you may seem like craziness to someone else – maybe even to your team
- ▸ **Repeatable** – because you want everyone in your team to do the same things in the same uniform way – consistently

That's what makes business systems effective. That's what you want your systems to be. That's what I want you to aim for. To have *Simple, Logical and Repeatable* (SLR) systems in your business that are so integral to the way you work that they become 'the way we do things round here', 'the way we operate', 'the way we roll'.

So SLR systems are what you're aiming for. How do you get started?

Routines

Start with your routines.

Think about those things that you do every single day and start with them.

Ask yourself how many of these routines you could hand over to someone else, today. You repeat every single one of them over and over again, but are they always completed in the same way, and to a consistently high standard?

Once you have your list of routines, to make them consistent you'll develop what we call 'How-Tos'.

How-Tos

A How-To does exactly what it says – it explains how to do a task.

It's a step-by-step guide, that explains how to prepare to complete a task; the steps you will follow to complete the task to the standard required; and why it's important to do it this way.

DAILY	WEEKLY		MONTHLY		YEARLY	
List the tasks you want the team to perform every day	List the tasks to be performed once a week, every week	Day of week	List the tasks to be performed once a month, every month	Day of month	List the tasks to be performed once a year, every year	Date

Simple

Your How-Tos have to be easy to understand.

So many people over-complicate their systems and add unnecessary bells and whistles which they imagine will make the system better. They don't. They just make it more complicated.

Sometimes a system can become complicated over time, often because too many people have been allowed to adjust it to suit their own way of working.

Sometimes it becomes complicated because we build in too many checks, because we don't trust, or we need to control.

Sometimes we've just become bored with doing things the easiest way, and decided to 'spice things up'!

Simple is good.

Anyone can follow a simple, straightforward How-To.

Logical

Let's be honest, we all do things that are completely illogical. They seem perfectly logical to us at the time, but to everyone else it's clear we've lost the plot!

For a How-To to be effective, it has to be logical. It has to be reasonable, and make sense to those who are going to use it, not just to you.

The best way to achieve a logical system is to use 'the five Whys'.

> ▸ The first *why* should always be 'Why do I have this system?' It may be a system that gets you from A to B – but is B really where you need to be going?

- Be sure that it's the right system for you/your business – something that makes life easier – before moving on

- If it is the right system, then check each step in your How-To by asking *why* four further times. 'Why do we need this step? Why do we do it this way? Why have we added in these steps... do they add value?, Why do we do this and not that?' and so on

Check your logic at every stage, and if you have a team, involve those closest to the task in developing your How-To.

Repeatable

You don't create a How-To for something that you're going to do once and never do again.

There was no need for me to develop a How-To for jumping out of a plane, for example, because much as I loved the experience (once the 'chute had opened), there is not a cat in hell's chance of me ever doing it again!

But you should have a How-To for anything that you're going to repeat, even if it's only once a year.

Record your How-Tos

How many times have you gone back to do something that you've done before, and you've forgotten how you did it? You have to go searching through Google, or trawl through YouTube videos to remind yourself of the best way to do it.

And then, even having gone through this pain, you *still* don't record how you did it to make it easier for yourself next time.

That R in SLR could just as easily stand for Recorded.

Are your How-Tos recorded and therefore useable by someone else? If not, take the time to record them and then store them where they can be easily accessed and used by you and the team.

A lot of business owners get hung up on the need for an operations manual, which sounds great – McDonald's had an ops manual of course, three inches thick – detailing how to do pretty much everything in the business.

But times have changed. You don't want or need a manual these days. You want something that's really easy to access, and that meets the different learning needs of individuals in your team.

Think about how you learn to do new things. If you're anything like me you'll Google it, and find a YouTube video that'll show you step by step.

There are lots of ways to learn these days – your How-Tos can be videos, marked up documents with an audio commentary, simple Word documents, PowerPoint slides – one size doesn't have to fit all.

And you can store all of your How-Tos in whatever format you choose, online – in a wiki, in Dropbox – again, there are lots of options for storage.

Working solo?

No real difference. You still need to make the way *you* do things simple, logical and repeatable. You still need to record what you do so that when you start hiring, your new team can hit the ground running, doing things the way *you* want them done, and to *your* standard.

It's all about making life easier. Yours as much as anyone else's.

It's the only reason systems exist.

HOW TO COMPLETE A MONTHLY STOCK ORDER

COMPLETED

1. To be completed on the first working day of each month. ☐

2. Open Monthly Order form on tablet/pc. ☐

3. Count stock as listed and enter the amount in the 'Stock-in' box. ☐

4. The spreadsheet will calculate the amount to be ordered and will record in the 'Order' column how much is to be ordered. ☐

5. Phone the different orders as listed on the order form, using the phone number provided. ☐

6. Pay for the order using the company credit card. ☐

7. Complete the 'Order placed with' and 'Order number' sections. ☐

8. Complete the 'Date completed' and 'Completed by' sections and finally sign. ☐

9. Save order form in 'Monthly Order' file under the relevant month's name. ☐

WHY DO WE DO IT THIS WAY?

It is important that we never run out of stock. If we do there are several things that could happen as a result.

1. The product may not be available that the customer ordered, therefore a potential loss of sales and the loss of a loyal customer.

2. This could affect our brand as dissatisfied customers often tell other people about their poor experience.

3. Staff may have to go to local shops to buy a replacement product, incurring an additional cost as the placement product will be more expensive, wasting staff labour.

By ensuring we always have available stock will mean a smoother business operation.

PROCESS IN PRACTICE

A while ago, we mapped out a customer journey for one of our manufacturing clients – we map it out on a roll of brown paper, looking at all of the touchpoints that the customer has with the team, and who is involved at each point.

Their journey was about twenty-five feet of brown paper long, and so confusing that my head hurt when we'd finished.

The sales team were involved from start to finish of this journey – I'm surprised they ever had time to sell – and the customer had to speak to four different people in order to do business with the team.

Supporting the journey there were four teams, all overlapping in terms of the roles they were performing, and all doing things in a very different way.

What had happened was what happens a lot in successful small businesses. They had started small – the owner and three trusted team members all of whom were very clear about their role and very focused on it. Of course, they quickly became successful, and with the success came a bigger team, and an even bigger team, until soon they were a team of thirty.

The way we do things around here had become confused, as each of the four original team members gave the new people their version of what the operating processes were. As a consequence, their service and delivery times were poor, and they were losing staff – almost as quickly as they could hire them.

Our job was to unravel it (always easier when you're not in the thick of it), to look for the simplest route for the customer, and the most logical way to support their journey.

As a result, their customer journey has shrunk from twenty-five to ten feet of brown paper; the teams, now clear about their roles, focus on delivering in a much simpler, more logical way; and customers get a much more efficient service. It's still a work in progress, but together we are making progress and that's the key.

So again, think about your business. What you will change or do differently to improve, 'The way we do things round here'?

FOUNDATION #2 TOP 5 TAKEAWAYS

1. It's crucial that you view your customer journey through your customers' eyes; through their very real experience.

2. Some of the touchpoints with your customer are more critical than others. These are your Moments of Truth.

3. You want your Journey to be as simple and straightforward as possible for your customers. Friction-free. Easy to do business with.

4. Think of your operating process simply as 'The way we do things round here', and make the way you do everything, Simple, Logical and Repeatable.

5. How Tos explain how to prepare to complete a task: the steps you will follow to complete the task to the standard required and why it's important to do it this way. They can be videos, marked-up images or simple Word documents.

FOUNDATION #2 MY ACTIONS

Priorities

1. _____

2. _____

3. _____

Do one thing

The baby step I'll take TODAY is _____

_____

_____

_____

_____

CHAPTER 4

Foundation #3 People

Who's coming with me?

Building and developing your high performing team

If you want to grow your business, other people are essential, whether they are partners, associates or affiliates; whether you find them on Upwork or you employ them. If you want to grow your business without killing yourself, or if you want to replace yourself in your business, you will need people.

Many business owners shy away from employing as an option, 'Aargh! I tried that once and I'm not going down that route again!'

'No way! Far too much hassle.'

'You gotta be kidding me – I can do the job better and quicker myself.'

Others who have employees are either struggling with, or hugely frustrated by, the whole experience:

'I've told them a million times how to do this. Why don't they just get it?'

'I just can't get them to stop playing on their mobiles.'

'Why do they keep making the same mistakes?'

Maybe you recognise your own grumblings here.

When you think about employing people, my guess is that the words HR, legal and discipline spring to mind. The soul-shrinking, limiting side of employment! So I'm going to challenge you to adjust your thinking, to change your mindset.

When you think about building a team I want you to think:

▶ Helping individuals to fulfil their potential.

- ▶ Working with engaged employees who want to do a good job and take ownership – without you breathing down their necks.

- ▶ Running a consistently efficient business where you have control whether you're in the office or on the beach.

Because the truth is that if you have the right people systems in place, and the right mindset, employing people is not only straightforward, but also hugely rewarding.

By the 'right' systems I'm talking about your systems for hiring, for training and personal development, for performance management, for reward and recognition – the four essential people systems that keep everything in your business consistent and controlled, that keep every team member informed and engaged.

Remember – a system for everything in your business, just like McDonald's.

Because here's the thing. If you:

- ▶ only bring the right people – people who share your values – into the business

- ▶ show an interest in them and develop them as individuals

- ▶ give them all the information they need, and logical systems so that they can do the job to your high standards

- ▶ manage their performance – give them structured feedback regularly and consistently, making sure they know the consequences, good and bad

- ▶ recognise them and reward them for a job well done...

your business will grow, to whatever size you want it to, and without you needing to be there.

THINK OF THE FREEDOM!

And if you doubt what I'm saying, think again about McDonald's, or Virgin, or Apple.

It's not by chance that the average management employee at McDonald's has around twenty years' service, or that people want to work for Virgin and Apple.

Successful business is based on the strength of your employer brand as much as the brand you market to your customers.

Build your people systems, build your business.

So the third foundation of The McFreedom System® is all about getting the right people into your business, and giving them the information and support they need to run your systems effectively.

▸ BUILDING YOUR
HIGH PERFORMING TEAM ◂

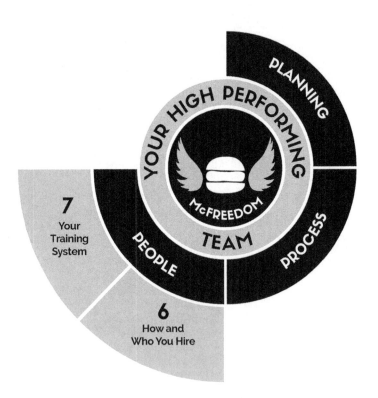

6. How And Who You Hire

'The main way to reduce stress in the workplace
is by picking the right people.'
JESSE SCHELL

The Decision – to hire or not to hire

When you're starting out in business, this one question can lead to many a sleepless night, and the choice you make can either stunt your business growth or get the business flying.

I don't know about you, but I agonised for months over my first team member. Could I afford to hire? Could I afford not to? Looking back, I knew all along that I was going to hire, it was purely a matter of timing.

As a successful small-business owner, it can become almost too easy to hire. You have the revenue, you have the cashflow, you have the immediate need – why wouldn't you add to your burgeoning team?

Well, just because you can, doesn't mean you should. Just because you have an immediate need, doesn't make hiring a good business decision.

As far as possible, your hiring will be strategic, focused and well thought-through. That's why you developed a people plan as part of your 3-1-90 so that hiring decisions are never last minute, made off the cuff, disastrous!

Yes, we've all been there – hired in haste, and left to repent at leisure.

My golden rule for hiring:

NEVER HIRE IN A HURRY.

The People Plan

When you developed your people plan (back in Foundation #1) you used three key pieces of information:

1. Your 3-year goals.

2. Your 'strengths, weaknesses and potential' chart for your existing team.

3. Your gap analysis revealing the gaps that you would need to fill through training or recruitment, in order to have the right people, with the right skills, in place when you needed them.

You focused on the big question 'What am I trying to achieve, and why?', so that any hiring that you planned would be focused on, and a requirement for, the achievement of one or more of your 3-year goals.

You then identified a gap in your team, made sure that no one in your existing team had the right skills now, or could be developed into the role – and made a strategic decision to hire someone new.

You're hiring on the front foot. Great start!

So, now all you have to do is hire the perfect person for your team, first time.

The search for the 'right' person – how to hire well

Just for a minute consider the planning that goes into a wedding.

It'll often start eighteen months out. You think of a day that will suit – ideally one that has the best chance of good weather, doesn't clash with any big sporting event, that sort of thing – and then you work back from there.

You write lots and lots of lists to make sure you cover all the bases. Only then does the real planning start – the challenges of the guest list, table plan, outfits, syncing the venue, the reception, the minister, the flower arrangers. On and on it goes.

They say that many people spend more time planning the wedding than they do planning the marriage, and it's way too close to the truth.

Thanks to your people plan, hiring a new team member may well be planned eighteen months or more in advance, but even if it's not, it should be planned with as much care, if you're going to hire the right person first time.

But what does this 'right' person even look like?

Well, their values match your own for a start, and they'll have all of the personal attributes that will see them easily fit into the way you and your team work; great work ethic, high energy, positive view of life – that sort of thing.

Their CV may well be great too, but you need to keep in mind that it'll only tell you what they have experience of, not how they did it, or whether they were any good at it.

Of course, if you're going to hire to your values, then you have to be really clear about what they are, and that brings us back to two of the key questions that we discussed in Foundation #1:

1. Where are you going?

2. What are the values you will live and work by?

When you're really clear about your values, you can use them to recruit the right people – the people who stand for the same things.

So, if two of your core values are say, 'making a positive difference' and 'passion for customers', you won't want to hire a salesperson who focuses on getting a sale at all costs. If you're all about 'making business fun', then you're not going to take on someone who struggles to find their personality every morning. You get the picture.

A great way to get the right people to interview is to put together a job ad that shares the following three pieces of information:

- ▶ The purpose of your business. Why you exist, who you serve, your long-term vision

- ▶ The purpose of the role. How it fits into the business, what value it adds to the whole, what success will look like in the role, and

- ▶ A pen portrait of the person who is the perfect fit; which gives any potential candidates a clear picture of the type of person you're looking for

You want this person to fit into your team and hit the ground running, so it's vital that they know in advance what that means, whether they can see themselves in the portrait you've given them. It's not about hiring Mini Me – you may be an ideas person needing to hire a detail person, for example – it's about being a good match.

Hiring and training cost a lot of money, and you want to get it right first time.

Yes, of course, you'll have a probation period, but you really don't want to have to let someone go because you didn't suss out up front that they didn't share your values, or that they don't have the right skills, and then pay to go through the whole process again.

The world is full of businesses who have the 'wrong' employees – people with the wrong skills, the wrong values, the wrong attitude, for the business they are in.

Whoever said the following was right on the mark:

'Development can help great people be even better – but if I had a dollar to spend, I'd spend seventy cents getting the right person in the door.'

How to make a first day memorable (for all the right reasons)

Even if it was only a part-time paper round, you've probably had a first day in a job. Can you remember what it was like? Whether you were over-awed, bored or just completely bewildered? Did you take in every word that was said, or did you go home on a caffeine-high with a numb bum? Chances are you came away thinking, 'Thank the lord that's over!', and that day two can't possibly be as bad!

A first day is your opportunity to make a great first impression. It's your chance to get your new team member excited about their future with you, to understand what's expected of them, and get a feel for what's possible.

To mis-quote the film *Gladiator*, 'What we do today echoes in our future'. What you do on their first day, will set the tone for their time with you.

Whether you had a great first day or not, think about what would have made it special? What would have got you buzzing? I'm pretty sure it wouldn't be endless facts and figures about the business.

The welcome

The first thing you have to get right is the day they are starting.

Sounds obvious doesn't it, but I could give you loads of horror stories of new starters showing up for a first day to be met with:

'Who are you?'

'Oh, you're the new guy. Right, well the person who deals with new starters isn't in yet, so if you can just grab a seat over there...'

'You're starting today? I thought it was tomorrow. Well I'm too busy today, can you come back tomorrow?'

You think I'm exaggerating don't you? Sadly I'm not. In fact one of those three happened to me, and you can imagine how it made me feel – deflated, unvalued, wondering if I'd made the right decision, take your pick.

Remembering when your new team member is coming in, setting aside time to spend with them, and being fully prepared to welcome them into the business, are first line requirements for getting your relationship off to a great start.

The welcome they receive from you and the rest of the team, that very first impression, will stay with them long after what you told them about the business for the rest of the day is just a distant memory.

The format of the day

There are some very basic things you have to get across to every new starter – where the toilets are, the fire procedure, where everyone goes for lunch maybe – but you want to keep these as brief and to the point as possible, so that you can focus on the things that are going to inspire them:

- ► The story of how you got started and the challenges you had to face (the short version!)

- ► Your vision for the future

- ► The culture of your business – what's important to you and your team

- ► The part they'll play and your hopes for them

Split their day into three short sections:

1. The things they must know – health and safety rules, holiday times, their probation period etc

2. The inspirational – as I've just covered, and

3. The practical 'get them started' stuff, so they can hit the ground running on day two

If you look at your content and think it's way too much to take in, then cut it. You want to avoid overload and get most value from their time, and your own, and besides, you don't have to tell them everything about your business on day one.

How you deliver the day should reflect you and your business. I'm not talking a song and dance routine, but their first day should be full of high energy, passion and creativity, and be as interactive as you can make it.

Get your existing team involved too – get them to do the 'tour of the business' (a walk round the office if you have one, or a tour of your website if you don't).

Ask one of the team to talk about their last great day at work and what happened? What they say and how they say it will tell your new team member more about your business culture than any list of bullet points.

If this is your first recruit, do something fun and interactive with them - take them to meet a customer, maybe. Whatever happens, don't have them sitting in the same chair, in the same room, all day.

You want them to be engaged, relaxed and enjoying themselves. You want them to go home buzzing, telling their family and friends about what a great decision they made to join you, about how much they're going to learn, about what a great team they've joined.

You'll never get a second chance to make that sort of a first impression.

Make their first day count!

Checking they're right for your team: what's a probation period all about?

Just like everything else in your business, your probation system will be clear, straightforward and professional, with supporting documents that tell your new employee everything they need to know.

Your memorable first day will have set the tone and set the standards for your new team member and inspired them to hit the ground running, to be an asset to your team from the off.

Probation is your fail-safe, a way of making sure that the person you've hired is the right fit for your business and vice-versa. Don't think it's all about your choice, they have a choice to make too.

A probation period has a start, and it should also have an end! Quite a few business owners forget that bit and leave their new team member to 'drift' into a full-time position without any measurement or recognition of having had a successful probation period.

Bad enough when they've been a success – even worse when their probation period has been really poor and they've shown what a bad fit they are for the team and the business. You let them drift, don't review their probation, and then, somehow, several years later, they are still with you, still causing problems, everyone knowing that they just don't fit.

It's so important to have a measured and well-managed probation system.

How to plan an effective probation

The length of a probation period will vary depending on your business, but for me, three months is the ideal – long enough to get a good feel for the new team member and how they work, and short enough to avoid 'drift'.

A really robust probation will include all of the following:

1. A memorable first day

2. Performance goals and measures
   Create a Performance Development Plan which covers the key areas that you want to measure during their probation period – perhaps things like speed of service, accuracy and also the more subjective indicators like cooperating with team members, ability to build relationships with customers etc.

3. Training for the tasks to be measured

   Your team member's initial training should enable them to complete tasks that they'll perform in their role.
   If a main aspect of their work is working in a team or dealing with customers, then you don't want them isolated with their head in a book. So tailor your training to give you the best indication in the timescale, of their future performance.

4. Time at the coal face (depending on your business and the role)

   McDonald's have always been very good at this; giving every new person a taste of the restaurant floor, the coal face – even if their role will never take them back there again. They want every new starter to know what the business is all about – to meet customers, and to work alongside the people who will serve those customers every day.

It's a great way of assessing whether someone really buys into the business vision and values.

5. Review and conclusion

At the end of their probation period, review their performance using the *One-Page Performance Review* that we'll discuss further in Foundation #4.

If you've worked with your team to measure and manage your new starter's probation period, by this point you'll know whether they're right for you and your business. You will know the 'critical fails' for your business – things that ring serious alarm bells, and make the individual a definite 'do not hire!' – maybe it's attitude to customers, or initiative, or even appearance. Watch for these 'critical fails' throughout the probation period, and end it early if you know that they're just not right for your team.

If they've been successful congratulate them, give them feedback on their performance and areas for improvement (as you would with any performance review) and welcome them to the team – making a big fuss of their success in front of their team mates.

If they've not been successful, let them go, positively: Give them pointers, if you can, that will help them to be successful in a role with someone else. Inspire them to find the right fit for them. Don't let them leave feeling a failure, but do let them leave.

Hire only those who fit

The benefits of hiring only the 'right' individuals are pretty obvious.

How many people tell you when they have something expensive to buy they'll get it from John Lewis because they trust them? And what's that trust based on? Thousands upon thousands of individual interactions between customers and John Lewis staff, that have been handled so well that those customers have talked to friends about them, written blogs about them, recommended that their family go there and, of course, they've gone back themselves.

Other businesses have got this sorted too, and stand out as a result: Apple and their knowledgeable and helpful staff; McDonald's, who give a consistent and reliable experience wherever you are in the world; Virgin Atlantic, who always look to make things easier, and fun, for their customers.

These are the sort of qualities that you want in your team, the sort of reputation you want your business to have, so it's important that you don't settle for 'good enough'.

Hire the right people for your team and your business – those who share your values and buy into your vision – and then train them.

7. Your Training System

'The only thing worse than training your employees and having them leave is not training them and having them stay.'

HENRY FORD

Training is something that McDonald's are renowned for, and rightly so. They invest loads of time, money and effort into training every team member from the restaurant floor, right through to senior management on the board. Your development at McDonald's doesn't end. It's not a 'done once and that's it done' sort of thing. It's ongoing development of you as a person, as well as an employee.

For me, it's the way training should be done, not least because it's great for business.

Two of the questions I'm asked most often are, 'How do you get a teenager who won't even tidy their room to perform to any sort of standard in a business?' And, 'How do you get people to do what you want them to do in the way you want them to do it?'

It's something that McDonald's have always done exceptionally well – take a young person, quite often someone that the education system has 'disagreed with', and within weeks, if not days, have them performing a task to a high standard, as an essential part of the team.

I saw this over and over again at Macs. A moody, or often painfully shy teenager joins the team, they're taught how to manage an area in the restaurant, maybe the fry station, to a high standard – and, before you know it, they're taking pride in both the quality of their products and the cleanliness of their area, determined that no till person will be waiting for fries on *their* shift!

It's impressive, but it's not rocket science.

And it doesn't just work for simple tasks like cooking french fries or flipping burgers (although in my day, when burgers were flipped, there was a definite art to it), it works for higher level activities and management development too.

I was a restaurant manager at twenty-one, naive and with limited previous work experience, working with two assistants who were eighteen, and in sole charge of a £1m+ restaurant, managing a team of thirty. I'd like to think the three of us were very talented, but even had we not been, we were given the training and development to manage the systems and the team, that ran the restaurant.

Teach anyone to do anything to a high standard, check in on them regularly to make sure they're maintaining that standard, then give them ownership and watch them fly.

Training and personal development work. They're an investment with a massive return. McDonald's are your evidence of that.

Train your team to run your systems

If you want your business to continue to grow, and to provide consistently good standards for your customers, you have to do two things: systemise your operation and develop your people to run your systems.

So a good training system that covers both essential skills for your business and personal development for individual team members, is essential.

You've already invested time in hiring the right team member, so now, when you spend time and money developing them, you can be pretty confident it's going be a long-term investment.

The savings you'll make from not re-hiring and not re-training will certainly far outweigh the cost of developing the right team.

Your training system will be made up of three parts:

1. Initial training

2. Ongoing/role-specific training

3. Personal development

Initial training

Regardless of the role, it's always a good idea to have an initial training plan for every new team member that will guide them through all the basic areas of your business – those areas that you want your whole team to understand and operate at some level.

You're going to have a good idea of how long this initial training period, including time for the employee to practise and become confident in each area, will take.

Ideally, you'll give them a schedule which plots their initial training, and also develop a spreadsheet that keeps an ongoing track of progress and logs training completed for every team member.

Ongoing/role specific training

The more you invest in your team, the more value you'll get back, not only in terms of their performance, but also through their engagement with your customers and their loyalty to your business.

Continue to teach them new skills. Move them to different areas of the business. Look out for particular strengths and aptitudes and build on them. As far as possible, make your team multi-functional and flexible – they'll love the variety, and you'll always have cover when the need arises.

How to train 1:1

I bet you've had a mixed bag of trainers in your time; I know I have.

The ones who sit you down, tell you to watch what they do, rattle through an explanation at 100mph, then get up and leave you to it with an 'Ok, got it?' are my particular favourites.

Others have been great at training to a big group, really quite inspiring, but struggle really badly when they're asked to do the same 1:1.

What is it about 1:1 training that people find so difficult?

If you have developed How-Tos for every regular task in the business, they'll form the basis of your training. They will give you all the steps that you need to teach, and also the reason that the task is important to the business.

Then, it's a case of using your ABC training system – the 1:1 training system that McDonald's have used successfully for as long as I can remember.

Here's how it works:

- ▶ A is for Attention – grab it!

- ▶ B is for Breakdown – break the task down into bite-size chunks.

- ▶ C is for Check – make sure they've got it!

Attention

If you want your team member to be listening to what you have to say, concentrating so that they understand, and focused so that they are able to act on what they've learned, then you need to get their attention, and keep it.

There are plenty of ways you can do this, but if you're struggling, try one of these:

▸ Find out what their existing knowledge is by asking questions – you don't want to be going into detail with stuff they already know

▸ Tell them something interesting about the task they're going to learn

▸ Tell them a key fact, a funny anecdote, or a tale of disaster

▸ Tell them what the benefit of learning this task is for them

▸ Let them know how this task fits into the big picture of your operation

Keep your voice energised and be enthusiastic; it will rub off on them.

Breakdown

Make sure that you're prepared whenever you're going to do a piece of training. Get out your How-To guide and decide if the task can be taught in steps (for a simple task) or broken down into bigger chunks (for a more complex task) of several steps – like building blocks.

Walk your trainee through one chunk at a time – give them their own copy of the How-To so that they can see all the steps that make up each stage, and that they can review at home or as needed, until they are fully confident.

Think about your pace – too fast and they'll flounder, too slow and their minds will wander.

Get interactive when you can too, to keep them engaged. You might make a statement and then ask why. 'When you get to this point you do this. Why do you think that is?'

This can also be a good indicator of how well they are following what you're saying and if they're making links between one part of the How-To and another.

At the end of each chunk on your How-To, write, 'Check understanding' to remind yourself to do just that.

Check

After every bite-size chunk and once you have been through the whole How-To guide, check that they've learned the key elements by asking them a few testing, open-ended questions, starting with What, Why, How or When.

If they can't answer the questions, go back to the breakdown and re-train each section until both you, and they are confident that they've nailed it.

Then, when you've finished, let them practise.

Your training session might run something like this:

> **Attention:** 'Hi John, this morning I'm going to teach you how to take a customer's order. When I first joined the business, we were only taking about three orders a day, but now we are up to fifteen most days, and with you on board I'm sure that figure will grow even more!'

> **Breakdown:** 'OK, so the How-To for taking an order is broken down into seven different stages. Let's start with how we answer the phone, which sets the tone

for the whole conversation with the customer. The very first thing we do is... '

Check: 'Well done, John, you seem to have picked that up really well. Before we set you loose on a few live customers, let's just check how much you've remembered. No looking at your How-To.'

While very simple, this method of training works in the majority of situations, regardless of the level of the individual, or how complicated the task is – and if done well it doesn't need to be repeated.

Develop the person

As the leader of a team you have a real responsibility to develop the behaviours of the person as well as the skills of the employee, to help them to fulfil their full potential, and achieve their own personal ambitions.

You want them to behave in line with your values, the values that they share, and sometimes you'll need to help them to see when they are misaligned, and give them individual input and attention. For example you may have someone who struggles to be part of a team, or who is poor at written communication, or who is lacking in self-esteem.

Helping them to improve in these areas will not only help them to grow and develop as a person, but will also have a positive impact on your business.

Business is a team sport

Business is a team sport, and in team sports you'll often hear people say – well, they don't have the best individuals, but they definitely have the best team.

Building a great team is all about having the right blend, people who buy into you as leader, and the vision you set out for the business – people who share your values.

It's all about the care you take in hiring the right people for your business, first time; and then it's about training them – teaching them in great detail how we do things round here, developing the person as well as the employee – giving them all of the information they need to take ownership of their role.

Think of a Formula One pit stop team – think about how slick, how consistent those guys are; think about the trust placed in them to get it right.

Do you think they get training first? Do you think they are drilled until they can do their job perfectly, and at speed? Do you think they feel ownership for their job in the team?

Ownership is so important. When you give ownership to an employee you do two things; raise their confidence by trusting them to do a great job, *and* free up your time.

Beware of accidental managers

One of the biggest challenges you face as a successful small business owner is managing your growing team.

So, to make your life easier, what do you do? You pluck your very best person from the comfort of a job they excel at, and promote them to the lofty heights of management.

Fabulous! Reward for their great performance, and a signal to the rest of the team that there is potential for progression within your business.

But then what happens?

Reality sinks in, and without any training or coaching your highly-motivated new manager begins to flounder. The team begin to lose confidence and the mutterings start around the coffee jar. Your new manager goes from loving their job to dreading coming to work.

Sound familiar?

It's a sad truth that managers are less likely to receive training than any other type of employee.

Recent research found that a huge 71% of businesses don't train their new managers effectively, if at all; managers who have responsibility for developing team members, measuring performance, maybe controlling a budget and other resources to deliver results for the business. Scarily that means that a hefty percentage of businesses are being run by managers simply flying by the seat of their pants.

I'm sure the natural leaders and gifted organisers will thrive on the challenge, but what about the rest?

Those who are 'consciously incompetent' have a chance of improving – they'll recognise their shortcomings and do what they need to, to develop the skills they lack.

The dangerous ones are the 'unconsciously incompetent' – those who think they know what they're doing and plough on regardless: a downward spiral of the ignorant leading the ignorant. The damage they can do to your team, and your business is immeasurable.

Give your managers a chance to be the second line you need them to be. Focus on their training and continuous development, and they will do the same for your team.

If you want help with this, check out the McFreedom Managers Club at www.mariannepage.co.uk *– created to develop the second line managers of people just like you.*

One final word on management training. Some highly productive and talented people are not suited to management, or simply don't want to be managers, so be prepared to build a development plan for them that isn't a management ladder.

Training is an investment, and a big one at that, no question. But the return it delivers both to your bottom line and to your time freedom, makes it worth every penny and every minute it takes.

PEOPLE IN PRACTICE

There are lots of examples I could share with you about having the wrong people in your team, it's a frequent problem sadly. But I'm going to share just two, which highlight the most common causes of people pain.

When I started working with Amit, it was clear that he had a problem with the team. For a start they didn't work as a team, and they were all way too focused on the clock – never a good sign. Turnover was high too; for a business that was five years old, 90% of the people that I met had been there for less than twelve months.

There was one employee though who was driving Amit mad; always turning up late, questioning every decision, doing sloppy work; Amit was at his wits' end, and wanted to know what I would do about it.

'Well tell me one thing first', I said, 'Do her values match yours?'

'Good god, no!' was the reply, 'But she had an excellent CV'.

That is so often the problem, and one that you'll have difficulty overcoming. Hiring to a CV, focusing on the experience that an individual has had, rather than their values, their attitude, their fit for you, and your team, is a big, and a very common mistake.

So, Amit sat her down and had a conversation about his vision and his values, and what he was looking for in the people he worked with. He inspired the lady in question with his passion and drive, and she is now a real advocate of the business and a highly valued member of his team.

Focus on values – find those whose values match yours – you can always train for skill.

With Geoff, the problem was different; he'd been with Martin from the start, and had worked hard to help him grow the business. As a result, he'd been promoted to manager – reward for all his efforts. Well financially anyway. The day-to-day reality felt more like a punishment.

Plucked from a job that he excelled in, and where he felt completely comfortable, even when the pressure was on, he now found himself managing a team of fifteen – actually no, not even a team, a group of people who came together every day to work under the same roof. Their work standards certainly didn't match his; 'sloppy' and 'slow' were the two words that summed them up for him.

When I met him he was exhausted, frustrated and disbelieving that this group of people would ever do their job right without him watching over them, let alone take ownership. He was checking every piece of work that went out to clients, working longer and longer hours to do so, and the team, knowing their work would always be checked by him, didn't bother to check it themselves. Why bother if he didn't trust them?

Together we set to work on reviewing the customer journey with the team, I introduced them to the concept of *simple, logical, repeatable,* and we streamlined their flow of work – removing all of the hoops that they and their clients had been jumping through. We developed How-To guides for the most routine tasks, to achieve consistency and raise the basic standards, and we introduced regular meetings to improve communication – daily fifteen-minute huddles to set the expectations for the day, weekly meetings to review what had been achieved and set priorities for the coming week.

Once a month I got them to meet as a full team, and to have one of the team do a twenty-minute presentation on something that would be of interest and/or benefit to the whole team. After that meeting, I encouraged them to go out for a team drink, or maybe even a meal, to build team spirit.

With Geoff, I focused first on his mindset, and the notion he had that everyone but him was lazy, useless and not to be trusted.

I asked him to focus on training and feedback; to show individuals exactly what he wanted, by using How-Tos, and then to let them get on and do their job, without his interference. I encouraged him to trust that if he trained his people properly, and gave them feedback that encouraged them to improve, then they would, and that mistakes were not the end of the world, but a learning opportunity.

Geoff wasn't convinced at first, but to his credit, he did listen, and he did change both his mindset and his actions. The daily, weekly and monthly meetings became the norm, and as the team began to blossom, I watched Geoff relax into his role as their manager.

Twelve months later, with three further managers grown from the team, Geoff was promoted to Director within the business!

Proud or what?

FOUNDATION #3 TOP 5 TAKEAWAYS

1. Successful business is based on the strength of your employer brand as much as the brand you market to your customers.

2. My golden rule for hiring: Never hire in a hurry.

3. Hire people whose values match your own.

4. Training and personal development are an investment with a massive return .

5. Use your How-Tos to train your team and achieve consistency.

FOUNDATION #3 MY ACTIONS

Priorities

1. _____

2. _____

3. _____

Do one thing

The baby step I'll take TODAY is _____

_____

_____

CHAPTER 5

Foundation #4 Performance

Maintain your course and
increase trajectory

Leading your high performing team to create a high performing business

So you've built your plans, you have a 'way of doing things' that's *simple, logical and repeatable*, and that every team member gets because you hired well and trained effectively – you've done your bit, right?

Wrong!

You've built the machine, and it's running well, but if you don't keep it oiled and well maintained, if you don't update worn out or ill-fitting parts it'll grind to a juddering halt, stop working, start rusting. It needs regular, if not constant attention, power and capacity measured and monitored, slight tweaks and adjustments made to keep it purring.

In business terms, we're talking KPIs, systems reviews and your planning cycle.

In people terms, we're talking ongoing training, communication and feedback.

What we're really talking about is Performance Management.

- ▸ The oil in the machine
- ▸ The fuel that powers the engine
- ▸ The tracking that keeps the wheels aligned

Having invested so much in building your business, why wouldn't you invest just as heavily in having it run like a dream.

McDonald's put a massive amount of time and effort into oiling their machine. It's the fourth foundation of their enduring success, and the one that most successful small business owners neglect.

Performance Management is the real keystone of The McFreedom System®; the system that will either consolidate your planning, your process and the effort you've put into hiring and training the right people – or make it all a waste of time.

What gets measured, gets done. What gets managed, improves.

Your business needs to be kept on track. Your team need feedback.

Forget all the negatives – confronting, telling someone all the bad things they've done, making someone cry. Think about the positives – developing, inspiring, motivating.

Through ongoing, day-to-day feedback, backed up with more formal performance reviews and 'How's it going?' chats, your performance management system measures, manages, and continuously improves the performance of your team and the individuals in it.

Performance management is the difference between an ok team, and a highly engaged, high performing team; between a successful small business and a high performance business.

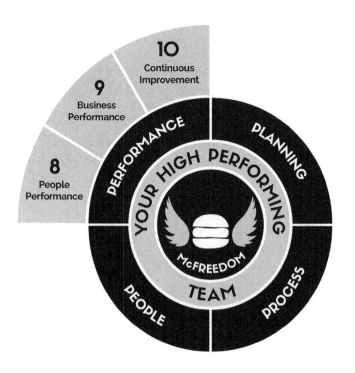

8. People Performance

"There are two things people want more than sex and money… recognition and praise'
MARY KAY ASH

Informal Performance Management, aka Feedback

What's not to love about giving and receiving feedback? It's the only way to help someone improve their performance, and it certainly helps you to improve your own.

Yet, generally speaking, it's not something we relish, and when we do give feedback, it's not something that we always do well.

Think about the last time you had a bad meal in a restaurant – what did you do about it?

A. Leave half your meal, and when the waiter asked how it was, say 'Fine thank you,' vowing never to return?

B. Give your waiter feedback – loud feedback that the whole restaurant could hear demanding that the cost be taken off your bill? Or

C. Ask to speak to the manager, quietly tell her the problem, and give her the opportunity to make amends?

I'm hoping your answer is C, but the truth is, for the majority of Brits, it's probably A – am I right?

Now think about how you give feedback in your business – how does that work?

▶ Is it a business tool you use to help you grow and develop your team?

- ▶ Is it a great big stick you use to beat them with every day? Or

- ▶ Are you the silent broody type that gives no feedback at all?

Feedback is essential in every business. You employ someone to do a job, or you give someone a task to do, then you must give them feedback either to correct something that's not up to standard, or to recognise them for doing a good job.

As Ken Blanchard, author of 'The One Minute Manager' put it, 'Feedback is the breakfast of champions', and deep down we all know that; deep down we all get that it's essential for any successful business owner wanting to build strong relationships and develop a high performing team.

But feedback is a funny thing – you either love it or loathe it depending on why you're giving or receiving it. We're all a bit weird about it.

I was discussing this very thing with my Masterminding buddies, and to a man they said, 'It's the confrontation. Nobody wants it. We're all too worried about the reaction, and how we'll deal with it.'

So we give someone a job, but then we don't tell them how they did? Did they do it well? Badly? At all?

I've lost track of the number of people who, when I've asked how they know if they're doing a good job, have replied, 'Well if nobody shouts at me, then I'm doing ok'.

It's leadership 101. No feedback, no high performing team. Simple as that.

Types of feedback

There are four different types of feedback, two that will have a really positive impact on your business, and two that will lead to it being sabotaged at every opportunity.

Let's do the bad guys first.

Negative

This is the one that should never be used, but is probably used most often!

Negative feedback makes it very clear that a job hasn't been done well, but doesn't explain what needs to be done differently to get it right next time.

Your team member doesn't know what they need to improve on, so they can't perform to a higher standard and, worse still, they're often left feeling completely demotivated, properly cheesed off, because it's been given in a very loud voice and in front of other team members.

No feedback

When you don't give any feedback to your team, you deprive them of their Blanchard breakfast – and prevent them from ever becoming champions in your business.

Like sending someone to Coventry (completely ignoring them), giving no feedback can also be incredibly damaging, and turn a highly motivated employee into one who thinks, 'Why should I bother – he won't check anyway'.

So, they are the baddies, let's learn about the goodies, and how to use them effectively.

Appreciative

This is the type that most of us enjoy, because it's the sort you give when a task has been done as you wanted it to be.

To really hit home, it needs to be specific, and ideally given in front of other team members. Why?

Because thanking a team member for a job well done in front of their team mates will

1. Make them feel really good about themselves, and

2. Show the rest of the team what 'a job well done' looks like, so that they can repeat the task to the same level.

Appreciative feedback is as much a development tool as a way to recognise good performance.

Constructive

Constructive feedback is used when you've asked for a job to be done, and it's not been done to the standard you wanted. The feedback you give to the individual, or team, will explain how it needs to be done differently next time.

It still needs to be specific, and unless it's team feedback, given on a 1:1 basis and away from everyone else, because you want your team member to go away thinking about how they're going to do a better job next time, not about how you've just embarrassed them in front of their mates.

If you get this right and offer your support, they'll be motivated and keen to do the job to your standard next time.

You want to build a high performing team, where individuals grow and flourish? Then if you ask someone to do something, make sure that you follow-up and give feedback, no matter how busy you are.

Don't skip breakfast!

How to give effective feedback

At McDonald's we were taught to give feedback in a very specific way. In The McFreedom System® we call it the EEC model, and it's very slightly different, depending on whether you're giving appreciative or constructive feedback.

For Appreciative feedback, EEC stands for:

Event	What did you ask the employee to do and how did they do it
Effect	What effect did how they performed the task have on you, on the team, on the business?
Continue	Carry on doing a great job. Reinforcing good behaviour.

So for example, you want to give feedback to an employee who's just answered the phone.

Event	Gail answered the phone

Effect	The customer will have felt welcomed, and you're happy with that
Continue	Keep it up

Like this, 'Well done Gail, you answered the phone really well there. You made the customer feel welcome, you gave your name to make it personal, and I could hear the smile in your voice. Great job, keep it up.'

For Constructive feedback, the C becomes Change.

Event	What did you ask the employee to do and how did they do it
Effect	What effect did how they performed the task have on you, on the team, on the business?
Change	What do you want them to do differently to meet the required standard.

'Karl I've just listened to you answering the phone. You answered it within three rings which is great, but remember to use your name to make it more personal and warm, like this, 'Good Morning Acne Consulting, you're speaking to Karl, how can I help you today?' And let's hear that smile in your voice. We want the customer to want to do business with us, so we need to make them feel really welcome.'

Constructive feedback is always focused on the bit of someone's performance that you want them to change or improve – giving them all of the information they need to do just that.

Effective feedback motivates your team to continuously develop and improve their performance. So make it inspiring and motivational, and give your feedback straight away, or as close to the 'event' as possible, to have maximum impact.

Like everything else that's good in your business, make the giving and receiving of feedback 'The way we do things round here', focused on helping every team member to improve their performance.

Do it well and it will help you to build a high performing and highly engaged team.

Formal performance management

If you've mastered the art of regular, ongoing feedback with your team, then your formal quarterly or six-monthly reviews, will simply be a pulling together of this ongoing informal feedback, recognising excellence or identifying areas for improvement, and agreeing the way forward.

No one should ever feel anxious, because nothing should ever be a surprise. Day-to-day feedback will have made it clear to the individual exactly where they stand.

As performance reviews are all about enabling progress – inspiring and motivating your team to strive for continuous improvement – it makes you wonder where the fear comes from.

Maybe it's from seeing performance reviews as confrontational – I'm going to tell the individual everything they've done wrong, and they are going to be defensive and argue back.

Or maybe it's because you've avoided giving that ongoing feedback; you haven't corrected a behaviour that's now going to come across as a much bigger deal than it needed to be, because your feedback will be a surprise to them.

Maybe it's because you haven't actually been monitoring or measuring the individual's performance, and your feedback will be very flaky and subjective, as a result.

Or maybe it's because you've had no training in performance management, and know that you'll be 'winging it'.

How to set up for an inspiring review

When you're first pulling together your performance management system, you need a few things to hand:

- ▶ Your 3-1-90 plans, complete with Focus Areas and SMART goals for both your team and individuals

- ▶ Your values one-pager, which explains what your values are, and the behaviours that are expected

- ▶ Your critical and key performance indicators (see business performance management)

- ▶ A draft one-page performance review document, like this example from one of our clients (below)

NAME _____		REVIEW PERIOD _____			
Performance Reviews exist to celebrate the areas in which you excel, or perform well and to dicuss how best to improve those areas which require improvement. Performance development is your personal responsibility. We're here to support you and encourage you not only to achieve the standards expected, but to fulfil your full career potential.					
Business Assessment	Excellent	Good	Satisfactory	Needs Improvement	Unsatisfactory
Demonstrates professional competency and knowledge in day to day work	☐	☐	☐	☐	☐
Takes full ownership for, and builds strong customer relationships	☐	☐	☐	☐	☐
Completes all work accurately and on time	☐	☐	☐	☐	☐
Follows daily routines consistently	☐	☐	☐	☐	☐
Pays particular attention to proactive communication with customers	☐	☐	☐	☐	☐
Applies training and uses initiative to pre-empt/resolve issues	☐	☐	☐	☐	☐

	Excellent	Good	Satisfactory	Needs Improvement	Unsatisfactory
Enters all appropriate information accurately into filing system	☐	☐	☐	☐	☐
Takes ownership of personal development	☐	☐	☐	☐	☐
Time Management & Personal Organisation Assessment	**Excellent**	**Good**	**Satisfactory**	**Needs Improvement**	**Unsatisfactory**
Achieves customer turnaround times consistently	☐	☐	☐	☐	☐
Sets and regularly achieves challenging personal targets	☐	☐	☐	☐	☐
Responds to customer e mails/ telephone messages within 4 hours	☐	☐	☐	☐	☐
Manages workload well to deliver on targets	☐	☐	☐	☐	☐
Asks for help if needed to achieve deadlines for customers	☐	☐	☐	☐	☐
Team Contribution Assessment	**Excellent**	**Good**	**Satisfactory**	**Needs Improvement**	**Unsatisfactory**
Communicates well with other team members	☐	☐	☐	☐	☐
Is a positive influence on the atmosphere within the team	☐	☐	☐	☐	☐
Keeps teammates motivated when the pressure is on	☐	☐	☐	☐	☐
Helps other team members when needed	☐	☐	☐	☐	☐
Shows a desire to achieve the best possible outcomes for our customers	☐	☐	☐	☐	☐
Communication is clear and consistent (oral and written)	☐	☐	☐	☐	☐
Listens effectively and asks for clarification when unsure of what is required	☐	☐	☐	☐	☐
Overall Assessment	☐	☐	☐	☐	☐

Additional Feedback

Reporting Manager Signature _____ Employee Signature _____

As in this example, your one-page review should be set up to assess an individual's performance in three key areas:

1. **Business Assessment**

   This section looks at the individual's contribution to the business; the skill they have shown in completing their work; the achievement of standards and achievement of targets; how well they have followed your How-Tos in the completion of their day-to-day work.

2. **Time Management and Personal Organisation Assessment**

   This focuses on their ability to manage their personal time to get things done and achieve targets. It looks at their ability to manage their workload; their consistency in delivery to time and on budget.

3. **Team Contribution Assessment**

   This section is all about how they go about their work; the behaviours that demonstrate their values; their ability and willingness to communicate; how much they contribute to the well being and performance of other team members.

Use this template as your guide, but make the review right for your team. You may even need to have a few versions to make it appropriate to different roles, or different areas of the business. On the whole, though, keep it as general for the whole team as you can.

On the reverse of the review, you'll set up team and personal targets, listing those areas that you will measure, and the results you expect them to achieve.

So, for example:

> ▸ You may have set a target to complete ten sales calls a day. Have they met this target?

▸ You may want them to answer any customer query within four hours. Have they done this consistently?

▸ Have they met your quality standards? Maybe entering information accurately into your system?

You'll know better than me what these team and individual targets are, so enter them, ideally in table format, on the reverse of your one-page review.

Something like this:

Management KPIs					
	Deadlines met	% Sales calls converted	Average Net Promoter Score for your Clients	Number of client complaints	Number of blogs posted
Target	100%	30%	8/10	0	4
Year					
Month					
Month					
Month					
Month					

The simple act of doing this, and communicating to the team how the formal review system will work, will focus everyone on these targets, and improve how well they are achieved.

Once you have your system set up, and you're happy with your review document(s) then share it with the team, ideally face to face.

Explain the importance of performance management, the benefits and the challenges, how you'll continue to give feedback on their performance day-to-day, and that the formal review will be *their* opportunity to talk about their performance, to discuss how they can improve and where they need your support.

You'll talk about the frequency of formal reviews – quarterly/ six monthly – what they'll be measured against and so on.

When you're looking to bed in your formal reviews, I'd recommend doing one every month for the first three months, just to help you and the team to feel comfortable with the process. Then move to quarterly. The more frequently you feed back on performance, the better your team will become at hitting their targets, and feeding back to you about any blocks they are facing.

Set your review dates well in advance, and then stick to them!

And remember your values – demonstrate what's important to you, what you value, through your behaviours – stick to the dates, be on time, and don't allow interruptions.

If you want to enjoy stress-free reviews...

Here's what's really important:

1. Make ongoing informal feedback a daily habit. Praise someone who's done a good job; give constructive feedback to someone who hasn't met your standards of behaviour or in the performance of a task. Do it at the time, and the formal review becomes no big deal for either party.

2. Align all the feedback you give with your values – be consistent day-to-day and person to person.

3. Give the feedback real time, but also keep notes that will remind you of the great stuff and the not so great when it comes to review time. Encourage your team to do the same. You can then both prepare well for the review.

4. Make the time you schedule for formal reviews sacrosanct. Show how much you value them.

5. Give individuals the chance to tell you what they've done well and where they need to improve. People are often so much harder on themselves than we might ever be. Giving them a chance to come up with things themselves makes the dialogue all about improvement and support. Performance reviews are a two-way communication opportunity, and the most inspiring thing you can do, is listen.

6. Be honest, always. Don't duck issues. If someone's performance isn't up to scratch they should already know; as we've agreed – no surprises. Use the review to get them to think about the consequence of their behaviours by asking specific questions like, 'When you said that to customer X how do you think that made him feel? What do you think he will do as a result?' You want them to understand the impact of their below-standard performance on the success of the business, and also on them as an individual.

Don't let a rotten apple affect the whole fruit bowl. If someone doesn't share your values, or isn't able to match the standards you have set for the team, part company with them, without delay. Less stress for you and the team, and ultimately better for them too.

You get what you measure, what you focus on, and the behaviours and achievements you recognise and reward.

Stay true to your values, and your team will flourish.

Reward and Recognition

Your recognition and reward system is another vital factor in developing your high performing team, and it will be most effective when you link it to your Performance Management System.

That said, what you recognise on a day-to-day basis is just as important, because your whole team will pick up on it as the true measure of what your priorities are, and they'll focus on that priority too.

So, for example, if you talk about being customer-focused, but only recognise those who save you money or waste it, then your team will know that your real focus is money.

If you tell your team that the customer is your number one priority and then openly slate a customer who gives you negative feedback, then they'll know that your pride is more important to you than your customer's view.

If you talk about how important people development is to you, and then cancel a team building event or quarterly performance reviews because money is tight or you're too busy; you're sending a very loud and clear message to your employees, who will lose trust in you and become demotivated.

No-one is fooled by those who talk the talk, but don't walk the walk.

Consistency

As with all of your systems, it's important that you're fully committed to any reward and recognition programme before you start one. Be sure that it's what you want to do, that your people and your business will benefit from it, and that you'll be able to keep it going once you start.

Lack of consistency is often the downfall of good reward systems, and it's often a lack of consistency in how individuals within the team are rewarded that causes the problem. If you're going to give out awards, have consistent criteria for how they are won; make sure it's clear and simple and understood by everyone. Of course, you don't have to have a formal system.

Little things matter, a lot. Like knowing your team as individuals – that's right up there with the most important. Saying please and thank you – it may be second nature to you, but you want it to be second nature to everyone who works in your business – part of, 'The way we do things round here'. Thanking someone at the end of the day for the work they have put in for you, sends them home knowing that you noticed what they did and appreciated their effort. It gives them another reason to want to come back tomorrow.

Having a system for remembering birthdays and anniversaries, and then coming up with something personal to acknowledge the day – maybe letting the employee go early, or sending them flowers – will also cost you very little, and the payback will certainly be worth it in terms of increased loyalty and motivation. Don't make a rod for your own back with this one, though.

Here are **30 SIMPLE WAYS TO RECOGNISE YOUR TEAM** and make them feel valued:

1. Say 'Thank you'

2. Thank them in front of their team mates or a customer

3. Tell them what a positive impact their actions had on the customer/the business/you

4. Take them out for breakfast/lunch

5. Write a few words about them in your newsletter /weekly e-mail/blog

6. Give them a monetary reward or a voucher

7. Delegate an important task to them

8. Make them responsible for training others

9. Give them a monthly 'Graze' box (or similar) subscription for the next three months

10. Let them shadow you for a day

11. Give them specific praise immediately and back this up at their formal review

12. Buy them a box of Cadbury's Heroes

13. Play David Bowie's 'We can be Heroes' as they come into work

14. Let them go home early one day

15. Give them an extra day's holiday – maybe their birthday!

16. Have a team away-day

17. Have a team dinner and pay for taxis

18. Create a treasure hunt, with clues leading to Easter eggs, Christmas gifts etc.

19. Give them a handwritten thank you note

20. Give them a bottle of champagne on their birthday (to take home) or flowers/chocolates if they don't drink, or even a card

21. Give them tickets to a sporting event, theatre, cinema

22. Invite them and pay for them to join a local business network

23. Let them attend a conference in your place

24. Arrange an afternoon for them at a spa, golf course, cookery school

25. Sponsor them if they are fundraising – cyclists/ runners/ knitters etc.

26. Present them with a commemorative gift on their first, fifth, tenth anniversary working with you

27. Buy a mocked up front page of your local paper with an article about them and substitute the real one

28. If you meet their spouse, partner, parent, tell them how much you value their contribution to the business

29. Buy cakes every time the team hit a target on your business dashboard (see the next section – business performance)

30. Say something that makes them feel valued, every day.

Above all though – keep it simple, keep it personal and keep it consistent.

9. Business Performance

*'There are only three measurements that
tell you nearly everything you need to know
about your organisation's overall performance:
employee engagement, customer
satisfaction, and cash flow.'*
JACK WELCH

Don't follow the crowd

There are so many successful businesses out there, people like you, with great products and great people. Like you maybe, they've grown from a 'one man band' to find themselves with a team, a group of loyal customers and a pretty ok turnover.

Life should be good, but instead they've found that as the team has grown, so has their workload. What used to work well when they were small, now just doesn't and they've become less efficient.

Costs have gone up. Profits have gone down.

They have good people but they just don't trust them to do the job like *they* would and end up wasting time checking up on them and re-doing their work.

Without realising it, they've become a chaotic operation where everyone is going in roughly the same direction, but in their own way and at their own speed, when what they set out to be was a Formula One operation – a high performing team where everyone knows exactly what they are doing, how it fits into the bigger picture, and that they are responsible for doing it to a high standard.

That's the sort of operation that needs strong foundations. The sort of operation that McDonald's has built their success on.

As a successful small business, you need to know where you're inefficient and where you're duplicating effort, and how to tweak or redesign 'The way you do things' to make a real and significant impact on your team and your bottom line.

There are only four key areas in your business where you need to look – areas where you can either save money or make more money.

Firstly, there's your operation.
Is the way you work *Simple, Logical and Repeatable*?
Where are you duplicating effort?
How are you using IT to support your people, and is it the right IT?
Where is the crazy 'but we've always done it this way' system in your operation?

Next, your team.
Is it full of people who share your values?
What sort of training do you have in place?
How are you managing and rewarding performance?
How do you root out poor performers and keep your whole team engaged?

Thirdly, your service model.
Is it built around your customer?
Are you easy to do business with?
Are you giving every customer the sort of experience from 'introduction to invoice' that will make sure they come back for more?

And finally, your financial controls – the numbers that you are focusing on, the reports you are asking for.

Do you have that dashboard of critical information that highlights the areas needing your attention and keeps you focused on continuous improvement?

The average small business squanders around £2,500 every month through inefficiency and waste, and even successful business owners like you stunt their own growth by being far too busy working *in* the business to work *on* it.

> **DON'T FOLLOW THE CROWD.**
> **DON'T BE AVERAGE.**

Manage your business performance by fact

When it comes to managing our business performance, most of us have a gut feel for what's going on, but how often is that 'feel' based on isolated figures and one-off events that have no context around them?

We are often so close to everything that we can't see anything clearly; we don't have that helicopter view of our business that would show us the peaks, troughs, inconsistencies and trends.

Ask the owners of most small businesses if they know their numbers, and I guarantee that, to a man, or woman, they'll say yes, because to most business owners the only numbers that matter are the top line or bottom line numbers: turnover, profit, cashflow and costs.

Ask them to dig a little deeper and they are all too often stumped.

- ▶ How many new customers have you taken on this year?
- ▶ How many customers have you lost?

- How many of each product or service are you selling?

- What is your ROI for each product?

- How many of your customers pay immediately/7-14 days/ 15-30 days/30+ days?

If we don't know the answers to questions like these, how can we know what's working and what isn't; what's making us money, and what's costing us more to get out there than is coming back; what our customers love and what they hate?

There is a well-known business rule of thumb – I like to call it the 'energy -vs- profit equation' – that says:

- 80% of your money comes from 20% of your business

- 15% comes from 40% of your business, and

- only 5% of your money comes from the remaining 40%

So, for example, if we know that an area of our business is expending 40% of our energy and delivering only 5% of our profit, but we are using it as a loss leader, or because we know that the product or service will start slow and grow, then all well and good. It's a strategic decision.

If, on the other hand, we've diversified because we think that's how to grow our business, or because we've seen others making good money in a different area, and actually have no idea where it sits in the 'energy -vs- profit' equation, then we need to be taking a good hard look at those 80:15:5 ratios, and work out if these diversified products are worth the time and money we're investing in them.

Understanding this, knowing where you make your profit and where your energy needs to go to drive that profit, is crucial to your business growth.

Your gut has its place, in an emergency situation, or where you are under severe time-pressure; but at all other times, knowing the facts of your business, and managing based on what they are telling you, in tandem with your gut, will lead to sound business decisions, and bring you much greater long-term success.

You know where your business is going. You have your vision - your destination, and you have your satnav – your 3-1-90 plan, so you know how you're going to get there. Your route is all mapped out.

What you need now is something that keeps you on track, that measures and monitors progress, that picks up on danger signs.

Your business dashboard

Think about when you're driving your car – a quick glance at your dashboard gives you all the critical information you need about how your car's performing – do you have enough fuel, are the tyres properly inflated, are all the doors shut, are your indicator lights working – critical data that warns you of a potential or actual failure in the system, and gives you the opportunity to react.

What if you had a similar dashboard for your business?

What if you had the critical facts and figures about your business performance at your finger-tips? A dashboard of crucial information about areas of your business that are make or break – revenue, profit, team satisfaction, new customers, lost customers?

Let's make you one, shall we?

How to build your dashboard

1. Start with a plan.

   Decide who the dashboard is for, and how you want them to use it.

   You've heard of KPIs, and I'm sure you have plenty, but I want you to decide on the *Critical Performance Indicators* (CPIs) for your dashboard – those things that are make or break for the business if they're not right.

   The effectiveness of your dashboard will depend on your ability to keep it current, so make it easy on yourself – five or six CPIs maximum.

   Measures you may decide to include:

   ▸ Financial Performance: profits, profit margins and cash balance year to date

   ▸ Revenue/Sales: showing charts such as sales per day and sales of your top selling products/services, year to date

   ▸ Sales Team: to show you exactly how each sales person is doing: total sales, number of leads, close percentage

   ▸ Customer Service: number of complaints, number of referrals, net promoter score

▸ Product/Service Fulfilment: to show how many services and/or products you've delivered, percentage of on-time delivery

2. Group the information you're going to show logically, with measures relating to people, sales, revenue, work in progress etc., together.

Put your most important measure in the top left of your dashboard, where you would normally have your logo. Our eyes naturally travel from left to right and from top to bottom, so don't waste the best spot on your page!

3. I'm sure you'll have seen those giant thermometers put up outside churches to chart the progress of fund-raising for their new roof, showing everyone at a glance how much has been raised, and how far they still have to go to reach their target.

Your dashboard is your giant thermometer, and can have the same impact when you make it visual using charts and graphs. At a glance your team can see how they're doing against a target, what the trends are and how much progress they're making. It has a much greater impact than just reading about it.

4. Decide how regularly you're going to/need to update your dashboard. If you have a weekly managers' meeting, then weekly may be regular enough. In some cases, monthly may work better – choose whatever works best for you.

Don't bust a gut to get real time or daily updates unless you will take action on a real time/daily basis.

Your dashboard is all about *action*. It should be designed to get a response from the team, just like a warning light coming on in your car; but shouldn't cause you or them to have knee-jerk reactions to one-off events.

5. Make your dashboard the key document for discussion with your team and your managers. Anything that you measure and monitor will improve, so celebrate every win, every movement in the right direction, to encourage even better results.

6. Take the action necessary to improve results. Remember those marginal gains!

7. Review your goals, targets and Critical Performance Indicators every quarter as part of your 3-1-90 planning.

   Have you achieved a target and need to raise the bar?

   Have your priorities changed, and you need to move focus to a different area of the business?

8. Don't add to your dashboard; swap a measure that's become less critical, for one that's now a critical measure of your business performance. If you keep adding measures you'll end up with an unwieldy dashboard that makes no real difference to your business.

Stay on top of your Critical Performance Indicators, and focus your whole team on continuous improvement.

10. Continuous Improvement

'Excellent firms don't believe in excellence – only in constant improvement and constant change.
TOM PETERS

McDonald's and Continuous Improvement

McDonald's is a pioneering business – a business that is always looking to raise the bar, to raise standards. Their mission is to 'deliver the quality, service, cleanliness and value their customers have come to expect from the Golden Arches – a symbol that's trusted around the world'.

'If I had a brick for every time I've repeated the phrase Quality, Service, Cleanliness and Value, I think I'd probably be able to bridge the Atlantic Ocean with them,' said Ray Kroc who introduced the four core principles to the business which are still the focus of every McDonald's employee today.

Like all successful businesses, McDonald's never stands still. They are always looking to improve, always looking to innovate, always looking at the customer journey to see where refinements and enhancements can be made.

To quote Ray Kroc again, 'A well run restaurant is like a winning basketball team; it makes the most of every crew member's talent and takes advantage of every split-second opportunity to speed up service'.

From the supply chain, through to the team on the front counter, every employee knows it's their role to improve, to develop and to make marginal gains, week by week, month by month and year by year. Nobody stands still. It's part of the business culture.

There is a rhythm, a consistent beat to everything McDonald's do, and their planning cycle is key to this – keeping all of their Focus Areas moving forward, keeping everyone engaged and on track.

Every quarter, their planning meetings create space and time to re-focus – to review systems, research competitors, innovate, and try out new ways of working, new products, new equipment.

In my time at McDonald's we moved from flipping burgers on a flat grill, to having a clamshell grill that cooked both sides at once, shaving off vital seconds in preparation; where previously a restaurant would open at 10:00am and serve burgers, breakfast was introduced, with a whole new product range, serving a whole new market; fish and chips, and pizzas were trialled and ditched; salads were introduced; coffee to rival Costa and Starbucks was given massive focus; new uniforms; digital training tools; new faster till computers; greater rewards for performance and long service. And these are just the things that spring to mind.

McDonald's are continuously improving. It's how they do things.

Continuous improvement is a business necessity, because, to coin another Krocism,

'WHEN YOU'RE GREEN YOU'RE GROWING, AND WHEN YOU'RE RIPE, YOU ROT'

The McFreedom System® and continuous improvement

By now it should be no surprise to you that The McFreedom System® is not a 'do once and it's done' sort of system – the four foundations, and the ten factors that form them, are together, a continuous cycle of performance improvement. And as with any cycle, you keep pedalling or the wheels stop and you fall off.

▶ THE MCFREEDOM CYCLE OF CONTINUOUS IMPROVEMENT ◀

Put another way, The McFreedom System® is the beating heart of your business – so you want to maintain a strong and steady beat.

How to keep a steady beat

The beat of your business relies on three things:

1. **Your Planning Cycle**

   The planning cycle works for McDonald's – keeps them focused on continuous improvement – keeps them moving forward towards their vision; and when you are fully committed to your planning cycle, it will give your business that same great rhythm. How?

   ▸ By bringing your team together to refocus on the vision, to adjust course or hold steady

   ▸ By giving you the opportunity to revisit your values – are they all still relevant to you and to your business?

   ▸ By creating space and time to review the four foundations – looking for marginal gains, in your customer journey, in how you hire and train, in your team and business performance

   ▸ By keeping everyone in flow

   Your planning cycle ensures that your team will always have a route map to follow. They will feel confident that every 90 days they will have the opportunity to pause, re-focus and celebrate, before continuing the journey.

2. **Your Communication System**

   Closely linked to your planning cycle is your communication system which builds the day-to-day, week-to-week, month-to-month rhythm and keeps the beat strong.

   ▸ Your daily huddle to set the priorities for the day, and check in with everyone – are they comfortable with what they're doing and how they're going to do it?

► Your weekly meeting/managers' meeting to review the week – what went well, what lessons could be learned, how have the CPIs moved on your business dashboard?

► Your monthly meeting to focus on progress towards your 90 day goals

Meetings that are crucial to keeping everyone engaged and involved.

3. Your Routines

Routine is essential for that steady beat.

When your planning cycle is routine; when your communication meetings are routine; when you have 'get set-up for the day' and 'end of the day' routines – success lists that tell your team what you want them to do every morning, every evening, every week, every month – How-Tos that show them how to do every routine task in your business, and your own daily routine for maximum productivity... *Then* you will have a strong and steady beat in your business.

THINK CONTINUOUS IMPROVEMENT. THINK MCDONALD'S. THINK *YOUR* BUSINESS.

PERFORMANCE IN PRACTICE

In practice, performance management is very powerful.

When we first started working with Graham he only ever spoke to a team member when they'd done something that had particularly annoyed him.

He had performance reviews in the business of a sort, but they were really just a tick box exercise, and they were mostly done by his practice manager.

Other than an occasional rollicking, there were no consequences for poor performance, and his reward system was hit and miss to be kind about it.

So he had disillusioned high performers and a couple of the team who were getting away with murder. Turnover was also a problem.

When we began installing The McFreedom System® and brought in consistent performance reviews focused on key measurements that we'd agreed with him *and* the team, three things happened.

First, the high performers blossomed – motivated by the clear targets to aim for and the regular recognition of their work, they upped their game another notch and really began to shine.

The second thing that happened was that two of the poor performers jumped ship after the second formal review. They saw that reviews were going to be done consistently, and that there would be consequences for their ongoing poor performance and failure to achieve individual goals; they left the business, before they were pushed.

The third thing that happened was that the team members who'd been struggling to deliver, and were worried by the new targets and measurements of their performance, raised their concerns and were given more training, which helped them to raise their standards and their contribution to the business.

Win win win!

Think about how this could work for you – what you will change or do differently to improve performance management in your business?

FOUNDATION #4 TOP 5 TAKEAWAYS

1. Performance management is the oil in the machine, the fuel that powers the engine.

2. Give appreciative and constructive feedback every day – no feedback, no high performing team.

3. Formal performance reviews should be inspiring – motivating your team member to improve their performance.

4. Build a one-page business dashboard that keeps you on track, measures and monitors critical performance indicators, and picks up on danger signs.

5. The McFreedom System® is not a 'do once and it's done' system – it's a continuous cycle of performance improvement. As with any cycle, you keep pedalling or the wheels stop and you fall off.

FOUNDATION #4 MY ACTIONS

Priorities

1. _____

2. _____

3. _____

Do one thing

The baby step I'll take TODAY is _____

_____

_____

_____

CHAPTER 6

McFreedom

McFreedom = the freedom to choose whether
to scale, grow, sell or franchise your business...
or run it from a beach somewhere.

The choice is yours

Once you have your four foundations in place, then your McFreedom is completely in your hands – what you choose to do with it, how far you can fly with it, is down to you.

And down to what I like to refer to as

Your big MAC

- ▸ Your **Mindset**

- ▸ The **Actions** you choose to take

- ▸ Your **Consistency** in everything you say and do

Mindset

Your mindset has a huge impact on the success of your business, it can help you or hinder you, it can free or block your path, it can keep you stuck where you are, or help you to grow.

Your mind is such a powerful tool – you need to harness that power and keep it focused on what will make you and your business stronger.

Take the time to check your mindset around three key areas of your business.

1. Your People

Not that long ago I had an animated Facebook discussion with a bloke who told me I had to accept that, 'People who come to work for you are lazy, incapable of following instruction, and invariably untrustworthy', and that I was naive to believe anything different.

Well I must be naive then, because for me, anyone who sets off to build a team with a mindset like that is destined for a whole heap of pain, and very high turnover.

People generally don't come to work determined to be miserable or to make your life hell. Yes, some may just want to get through the day, or through the week, to enjoy their free time; but most want their brain to be occupied, want to be challenged, want to enjoy what they do; even those who have no ambition beyond making enough money to live, want to be doing something that they don't dread getting out of bed for.

What you believe about the people you hire, and how you demonstrate what you believe, will have a huge impact on how they work for you.

- ▸ Do you believe that they want to do their best, and will do their best with training and your support?
- ▸ Do you recognise the qualities they have?
- ▸ Do you respect them as individuals, as well as members of your team?
- ▸ Do you see the best in them, and accept the odd quirk or idiosyncrasy?
- ▸ Do you trust them to take ownership for their role?

▸ Do you act as if any mistake is a learning opportunity for the whole team?

▸ Are you building the culture of mutual trust essential for a high performing team?

In hiring only those who match your Values you're giving yourself a head start – after that it's all about helping each one of them to fulfil their full potential. Make that your mindset and your people will blossom.

2. Investment

How do you view investment in your business? Do you see it as a necessary evil, or welcome it as a requirement for scale and growth?

Investment in your people

▸ If you have the right mindset around your people, you'll naturally be comfortable about investing in them – investing time to hire and train people who share your values, paying good rates to reward them, having a consistent performance management system to develop them.

▸ Your people are your number one resource – invest in them, show them how committed you are to their training and development, and they'll pay you back with their commitment, loyalty and outstanding performance.

Investment in your own development

▸ How about your mindset around investing in yourself? You obviously read business books, but do you work with a mentor who challenges you? How about courses and programmes that expand your thinking and broaden your experience?

> ▸ Do your homework, get real clarity around what's *right for you and your business right now*, and invest in that.

Investment in IT

> ▸ Your mindset around IT should be to see it as support – how can I use IT to make 'The way we do things round here' easier? How can it support the way we work? Don't buy a really clever IT system and then try to make your business fit around it. Don't let the tail wag the dog!

Investment in equipment

> ▸ Are you keeping up to date, giving your people the best equipment to work with – the kit that's going to make you more efficient, and make your team's life easier?

Investment in yourself and your family

> ▸ How about those holidays? Are you taking them every year? Regularly? What's your mindset around taking quality time away from the business? Do you recognise it as time to recharge your batteries, re-energise your mind, give yourself the opportunity to see just how well your team perform when you're not there?

3. What's possible

Many business owners have the mindset that success has to be hard – that you have to make great sacrifices and defer spending quality time with your family and friends, until you've 'made it!'

Change that mindset now – because all that will lead to is broken relationships, resentment, and stress.

Yes, building a business is hard work, but remember that you're building a fulfilling life not just a successful business, and with the right team and the right systems in place, you can and you *will* have both.

Action

Once you have the right mindset, then it's all about taking the action that supports it.

There's a great line in the film Gladiator – 'What we do today, echoes in our future' – I like to change that slightly to 'What we do today, *creates* our future'.

Every action you choose to take today will move you in a certain direction – either towards your vision of your ideal future, or away from it.

Today's actions create your future.

So:

If you want a great relationship with your children when they're older, take the action today that will build that relationship.

If you want a loyal employee who takes ownership, invest time in them today.

If you want a systemised business that runs without you, start creating those How-To guides for your most routine tasks, today.

Your actions today are creating your future. Never forget that.

Consistency

If you want consistency – be consistent.

- ▶ Consistency in your mindset
- ▶ Consistency in demonstrating your values
- ▶ Consistency in driving towards your vision

Your team pay as much, if not more attention to what you do, as what you say. The consistency of your leadership day-to-day, is therefore a model for how you want them to behave. Think back to what we said about values – they are the compass that guides your decisions, actions and behaviour - you need to live them consistently every day if you want to build your culture around them.

Consistency is king – for your team, for your customers, for your business.

McFreedom Culture

We all want a business where our team are engaged and motivated to do a consistently great job; where they look forward to coming to work; where they celebrate business success with us and feel a level of responsibility when things aren't going so well.

So how do you achieve that? How do you build a culture of ownership and accountability in your business?

The truth is, that no matter how small your business, you already have a culture.

To date, it's been evolving as a result of your existing big MAC, and the day-to-day behaviours, words and actions, that your team have been observing.

Is that good news?

Your culture is the soul of your business. In an owner-managed business like yours, you are the heart and soul of your culture; you set the tone, you make the rules, you lead the way for your team to follow.

As we said in Foundation #1, culture evolves from the demonstration of values, and through consistent behaviours over time.

So your culture is built around your actions, your team's reactions and the truth about your business – what *really* happens – on a daily basis.

Your personal impact is huge, and that makes it a huge responsibility because your people watch you, they listen to you and they copy you.

As you grow, your team and your managers build on the example you set, and your business culture becomes a monument to the values and behaviours that you exhibit every day – a powerful force in your business that will be difficult to change further down the line.

Day by day, action by action, you build your culture.

Keep that in mind, and build something you can be proud of.

Creating a culture of ownership

> *'A leader is best when people barely know that he exists. When his work is done, his aim fulfilled, they will say, "We did this ourselves".'*
>
> LAO-TZU
>
> (*BOOK OF TAO*, 6TH CENTURY BC)

The first time I read this, I loved it.

Every time I read it I get goose bumps.

I can't quite get my head around the fact that it was written in the sixth century BC mind you – it makes my brain hurt. Especially as here we are in the twenty-first century, still trying to get to grips with leadership.

Makes me think of a course I once attended about leadership and communication, where they asked everyone for examples of the last thing their leader had said to them.

'Merry Christmas!', said one bloke.

Considering the course was in August, it clearly indicated a leader whose people barely knew he existed, but maybe not in the way Lao-Tzu intended!

I love what Lao-Tzu wrote, because it's what I believe too.

Even though nobody in one of my teams would ever have said that they didn't know I was there, I do believe passionately that the best leaders give their people the tools and the training, the systems and the development, the ownership and the support they need to deliver results with minimum interference – then get out of their way and let them get on with it.

So your mission, should you choose to accept it, is to do yourself out of a job, and free your people to get on with theirs, which is basically what Lao-Tzu was saying.

How great would it be if you could send yourself this letter twelve months from now...

Dear [your name]

This letter is to advise you that as of [insert deadline date twelve months from today], your services are no longer required by this business.

While your valuable input will always be welcome at our quarterly planning and review meetings, and of course you should feel free to pop in now and again for a coffee and a catch up with the team, you are no longer expected to play an active role in the business.

The reasons for this are as follows:

Over the past twelve months, you've worked hard to build a high performing team. You've focused on hiring the right people, who share your values, who have a positive can-do attitude, and who take full ownership for the role that they are performing.

You've developed simple, logical and repeatable systems in every area of the business, and recorded them so that the team can be trained to follow them consistently. As a result, every task is now performed to the high standard that you set, and every team member takes full ownership of achieving that standard, every time.

Our customers now love us, and we are building the business through their repeat custom, and their regular referrals. You've made it easy to do business with us, and achieved consistency for both our customers and the team, who receive regular ongoing feedback and performance reviews which inspire and motivate them.

You have developed a culture of trust, where we rely on one another, and our customers rely on us.

Everyone loves working here, and while you're a pleasure to work for, you are simply not needed anymore. I therefore respectfully suggest that you use your new-found freedom to focus on growth, to create, to enjoy time with your family, to explore; to do whatever you like quite frankly.

Please have your desk cleared by 5:00pm on [insert date], at which time we will be cracking open a large bottle of bubbly to celebrate with you.

Best wishes

-your name-

The Boss

Can you imagine how good that would feel?

You want that for yourself? Then act on what you're reading in this book and surround yourself with people who buy into your vision and take ownership for helping you to achieve it.

People who relish responsibility, who have ideas, who learn what their role is, and what standards are expected of them, and then set out to make the role their own. Those people who want to grow and develop.

You don't want those who wait to be told what you want them to do every day, who have no initiative, no enthusiasm and no personal goals. Those people will never replace you. They will keep you trapped in the long hours, lots of stress, cycle.

As a leader, you need to give every individual you hire the opportunity to be in that first group – to take full ownership for their role. And to do that, you need to give them four things:

- ► An inspiring vision, complete with a clear road map to achieve it

- ► A simple, logical and repeatable way of doing everything in your business

- ► Training that shows them how to do the job, plus the standards expected

- ► Performance Management that keeps them on track, challenges them to grow, and then acknowledges and rewards their contribution to the business

Give them this level of support, and they will say 'We did this ourselves'.

MCFREEDOM TOP 5 TAKEAWAYS

1. When you have your four foundations in place, then your McFreedom is completely in your hands.

2. Get your personal big MAC sorted – Mindset, Action, Consistency.

3. Your mission is to do yourself out of a job, and free your people to get on with theirs.

4. Surround yourself with people who buy into your vision and take ownership for helping you to achieve it.

5. As a leader, you need to give every individual you hire the opportunity to take full ownership for their role.

MCFREEDOM MY ACTIONS

Priorities

1. _____

2. _____

3. _____

Do one thing

The baby step I'll take TODAY is _____

_____

The Last Word

I know you have a successful business. I know you make good money. I know you love the business you created.

But I also know that you're frustrated; that you hate that you're trading your life for money; that you don't have the time to take the business where you know it can go; that you can't get away even for a week and completely switch off; that you're not free to do what you want.

I have a dream!

Who doesn't know that line? And who said it? And when?

Just a few words, that inspired an awful lot of action. Life-changing, world-changing action.

A dream did that.

These days, in business, dreaming has a bad name; it's associated with wishing and hoping, with pie-in-the-sky thinking and head in the clouds delusion.

Certainly not with action.

Just think about your own dreams for a second – not those weird ones you have at night – I'm talking about the dreams you have for your future – your ideal future.

That's what most of us dream about, don't we? Our ideal future – that place and time when we have achieved success – no matter what we consider that success to be.

A wonderful relationship with someone truly special.

A great connection with our kids.

A business that runs smoothly, without the long hours and the effort.

Financial freedom. Health and fitness. Making a difference. Leaving a legacy.

Aren't these the sort of things we dream about for ourselves? Feel passionately about?

Passion drives action.

Martin Luther King's dream, his passionate belief in a dream, drove massive action.

Your dreams can do that too...

How?

By focusing on them, getting clear about what you really want – what's really important to you.

By planning your life around your dreams and ditching all the 'stuff' that's taking you in the wrong direction.

By getting conscious about the decisions you are making day-to-day. And

By taking *Action* every day that moves you towards your dreams.

What you do today echoes in your future – it creates it.

What are you going to create *Today*?

TO YOUR MCFREEDOM

Next Steps

Register your book

First, register your book at mariannepage.co.uk/registermybook to unlock several exciting bonuses designed to support you in moving forward on your journey to McFreedom, including a discounted ticket to our McFreedom Secrets Workshop.

Sign up for the McFreedom Secrets Workshop

Take advantage of your bonus, and join us for the next available McFreedom Secrets Workshop, where you'll put some meat on the bones of the theory you've learned in these pages.

Book a call with me

Book a strategy call with me, where we'll discuss the outcome of your Scale or Salability Indicator (Find it here mariannepage.co.uk/getstarted), agree the areas requiring priority action, and develop a 'first steps' action plan.

Book me as a speaker

You may want your people to get that systems are important; or maybe you want your clients to get that systems are essential if they want to grow their business beyond the plateau they're on; or maybe you run a group that would be really interested to learn how McDonald's achieve such amazing consistency, and how they could get a bit of that for themselves.

Whatever your reason, I'm up for gearing my talk to your audience – to engage them, to make them think differently, and to give them information and tools which may just change their lives.

Visit mariannepage.co.uk/aboutmarianne to book me for your meeting or event.

Acknowledgements

Firstly, thanks to you for taking the time to read this book. I would love nothing more than for you to take action on what you've read in these pages and achieve your McFreedom.

Thank you, Daniel Priestley for your belief in me and my book, and for the honour of being your first Dent author. Thanks also to my publishers Lucy McCarraher and Joe Gregory for your continued patience with my writing foibles, and for bringing *Simple Logical Repeatable* to life in print.

Thanks to my wonderful partner in crime Peter Hall and his talented wife Annabel - your support, friendship and enthusiasm for The McFreedom System®, have helped make the writing of this book a fun and fulfilling experience.

Thanks to McDonald's and to all my friends there past and present. Most of what I know about creating systems and developing high performing teams I learned in your company. Great brand. Great business. Great place to have grown up.

Thanks to all my clients, friends and mentors, for the challenge, the sharing and the inspiration that continue to shape my thinking and develop me both as a business woman and a human being.

Thanks to my five fabulous sisters: you're always there and I hope you know that you're always loved.

And, of course, thanks to you Sas for your love, loyalty and laughter. You, Biskit, Teddie and Rumble keep it real and make it all worthwhile.

The Author

Marianne Page has twenty-seven years of senior management experience with McDonald's. Over an eight-year period she worked closely with more than 14,000 managers and franchisees to develop their management and leadership skills, and through her focus on continuous improvement and system development saved the business over £1m in her final year.

Marianne now works with six- and seven-figure business owners who are victims of their own, often rapid, success, and who are unable to extricate themselves from working *in* their business in order to work *on* it.

Marianne has a reputation for being inspiring and fun-loving, and for taking an area of business that most business owners are terrified of or at best resentful of, and turning it into something that is easy, enjoyable, and actually gets done.

Through her bespoke McFreedom System™, modelled on the four foundations of McDonald's Success – Planning, Process, People and Performance – Marianne gives the successful small business owner a blueprint for scale, growth and personal freedom.

Her complementary programme, The McFreedom Managers' Club, mentors and develops the 'second line' managers of her clients' businesses, in the understanding that these are the guys who will actually make the business work, or not.

Marianne's award-winning McDonald's experience makes her one of the world's most qualified experts on the practicalities of implementing simple, logical and repeatable systems in every area of your business, and developing your high performing team to run them.

During her time at McDonald's, Marianne developed a number of high performing teams of her own, and was recognised with two of the corporation's three highest awards for her achievements.

She is a passionate believer that systems run your business, and people run your systems, and has spoken internationally on the power of *People + Process = Profit*.

Marianne loves writing. Her first book, *Process to Profit*, was hailed by her clients as 'better than *The E Myth*'. She also authored the acclaimed *McFreedom Report*, and writes a weekly blog, *McFreedom Mindset*, available on her website www.mariannepage.co.uk

Printed in Great Britain
by Amazon